ACA 122
College Transfer Success

Published by CPCC Press
PO Box 35009
Charlotte, NC 28235
cpccpress@cpcc.edu

ISBN: 978-1-59494-055-2

Published and Printed in the United States of America

For additional information, you are invited to contact:

Alyssa Williams & Donna Housman
Central Piedmont Community College
P.O. Box 35009
Charlotte, N.C. 28235-5009

Tel: 704.330.6357 or 704.330.4854
E-mail: alyssa.williams@cpcc.edu or donna.housman@cpcc.edu
Website: www.cpcc.edu
            www.cpccpress.com

CPCC Press is a division of Central Piedmont Community College Services Corporation.

Copyright © 2013 by CPCC Press, PO Box 35009, Charlotte, NC 28235; 704.330.6731; www.cpccservicescorporation.com.

Table of Contents

AUTHORS

Alyssa Bethel Williams, MA is a faculty member at Central Piedmont Community College in Charlotte, NC. She has more than 17 years of experience as an instructor, advisor and trainer of adults in the public, private and community college sectors of higher education.

Her areas of collegiate experience include leadership development, career counseling, new student orientation, academic advising, residence life, Greek affairs, judicial affairs, services for differently abled students and programming.

She is a graduate of Tusculum College and received a Master's of Arts degree in Student Development for Higher Education from Trinity University. In her current role, she is an instructor and Discipline Chair for Career Assessment and Transfer Student Success courses as well as teaches College Student Success and College Study Skills courses. Alyssa has also trained adults in the corporate arena on effective leadership, team building, group facilitation, diversity and conflict mediation and resolution.

Donna Housman, MS is a faculty member at Central Piedmont Community College. She has over 20 years' experience in teaching and training adults in corporate, academic and public settings, focusing on leadership and management development, facilitation skills, self-awareness and team building.

She is a graduate of Wake Forest University and has a Master's of Science degree in Adult Education from Virginia Polytechnic Institute and State University. In her current role she teaches College Study Skills, Career Assessment, College Transfer Success and College Student Success.

She also previously taught English as a Second Language classes providing civics based ESL instruction for intermediate and advanced ESL students and served as an instructor for ESL Fast Track Teacher Training.

Acknowledgments

This textbook is a project that would not have been possible without the guidance, support, encouragement, feedback and contributions of many individuals. These individuals selflessly extended their valuable **assistance** in the preparation and completion of this **project**.

First, we are grateful to our students. Your commitment to your academic and career pursuits inspired us to pursue this project in a way that would have a significant impact on your matriculation. We endeavor to provide you with information and skills that will create an impetus for your successful transfer to a four-year college/university.

We would like to thank our proof readers, Owen Sutkowski, Adam Hypes, Kelly DeMarte and Maria Williams from the Central Piedmont Community College Transfer Resource Center. We sincerely appreciate your willingness to share your experience, insight and feedback. Your contributions were invaluable to this effort.

Also, we would like to acknowledge with appreciation, Erin Phillips and Stephen Lancaster from the Financial Aid/Veterans Affairs department for their assistance.

Finally, we would like to express our gratitude to the CPCC ACA Division. Your support and encouragement was essential to the development of this textbook. Thank you for being the catalyst through which we could express our vision. We are grateful to be a part of such a wonderful team.

We hope that this textbook will serve as an intrinsic framework that will enable students to address and take onus of both the conceptual and process elements of transfer admission and degree completion at a four-year college/university. Our goal is to promote the student's ability to embrace the integration of the academic and student support environments of a college to bring about successful degree completion and readiness for the professional arena.

Thank each of you for your contributions that have helped shape this textbook.

Alyssa Bethel Williams
Donna Dimsdale Housman

Introduction

Congratulations on making the decision to continue your education after your community college experience is complete. You have made a wise decision! Research shows that the higher your level of education the lower your unemployment and the higher your earnings will be.

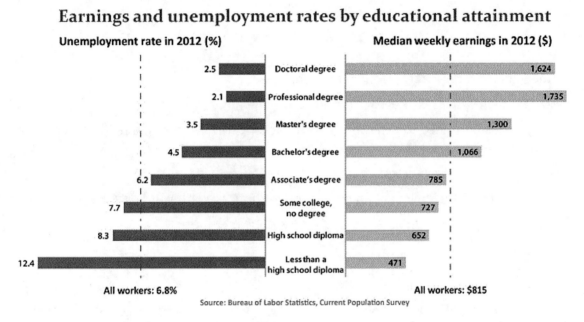

Earnings and unemployment rates by educational attainment

Source: Bureau of Labor Statistics, Current Population Survey

Today in the United States more than 45% of college students start in a community college (O'Shaughnessy, 2008). Here are some of the benefits of starting at a community college:

- The cost of attending a community college is less expensive than that of colleges and universities.
- The community college provides great experiential training before going to a four-year university.
- Classes are smaller and students can receive more individual attention.
- Students may be offered priority admissions to four-year colleges/universities.
- Great accessibility and flexibility allows students to live at home, work and save money.
- If necessary students can overcome academic deficiencies and get better prepared for college level work.

Many community college students are better prepared to go on to a four-year college or university after earning a two-year degree or after satisfying their general education requirements.

When a high school student decides to attend college, there is a defined process and plan in terms of college preparation and selection. But as a transfer student, there is not a "one size fits all" approach. Don't worry! In this course we will answer many of your questions and go through a systematic process to help you with the successful transition to a four year college or university.

The ACA 122 College Transfer Success textbook was created to assist students in their successful transfer from a community college to a senior institution. It will provide information and strategies necessary to develop clear academic and professional goals beyond the community college experience. Topics include the Comprehensive Articulation Agreement (CAA), college culture, paying for college, course planning, student affairs, career exploration, researching information on senior institutions, strategic planning, critical thinking, and communication skills for a successful academic transition.

Whatever your situation, this textbook will help you answer questions such as:

- When and how do I start planning for transfer?
- How do I know the best college to choose for my major?
- What things do I need to consider to ensure a proper fit for me culturally, socially and academically?
- What are the admission requirements to the school?
- Will they accept the courses I have already taken for credit toward an advanced degree?
- What financial aid or scholarships might be available to me?

Transferring successfully from your community college will require you to answer these questions and many others. You will have the opportunity to consider what college will meet your personal, social, academic, financial and cultural needs, which brings us to the objectives of this course. Students that successfully complete this course will be able to:

1. Demonstrate the basic skills necessary to research senior institutions for their career choice and personal needs.

2. Demonstrate ability to apply the NC Comprehensive Articulation Agreement and transfer resources to academic and career goals.

3. Develop an academic plan for successful transition to senior institutions.

4. Describe similarities and differences between two and four-year college/university cultures.

Throughout the course we will refer to the _5 Steps for Transfer Success_. They are listed on the next page and will be a road map to guide us as we move through the course.

The 5 Steps to Transfer Success

Step 1: Choosing the Right Major for Your Career
- Self-Assessment
- Choosing Your Major

Step 2: Understanding College Culture and Your Personal Needs
- Researching Different Types of Colleges / Universities in the US
- Exploring Your Individual College Needs
- Investigating the Best Colleges for Your Career Choice and Major
- Investigating Degree Requirements
- Understanding Course Planning and Progression

Step 3: Researching Finance Options to Pay for Your Four-Year College
- Exploring the Cost of College
- Investigating Different Sources Available to Pay for College
- Researching Ways to Save on College Cost
- Creating a Plan for Paying for College

Step 4: Creating a Personal Admissions Campaign
- Researching Admission Requirements
- Conducting Information Interviews
- Understanding Admission Requirements
- Conducting College Interviews/ Campus Visits
- Creating an Admissions Tracking System and Timeline
- Completing Your Transfer and Financial Aid Applications

Step 5: Making Your Choice and Making the Transition
- Evaluating Your Choices
- Identifying a Plan B
- Accepting your final offer
- Making the Transition Successfully

How to Use this Textbook

"The information contained in this workbook is essential to navigating the transfer process. No matter where a student is on their path to a 4-year degree, there are resources within this guide to assist and support their transition." -- Owen Sutkowski, MS, Director, Transfer and Career Services, Central Piedmont Community College

This textbook was developed to help guide you through your journey as you transfer from a community college to a senior institution. It will provide information and strategies necessary to develop clear academic and professional goals beyond the community college experience.

In this guide you will find narratives and exercises to walk you through the specific steps of choosing your major, understanding college culture, researching the prospective colleges and then making your choices. There are also references to online resources and books that will be useful in your process.

We hope this textbook will be a close companion as you work your way through this course and this life decision.

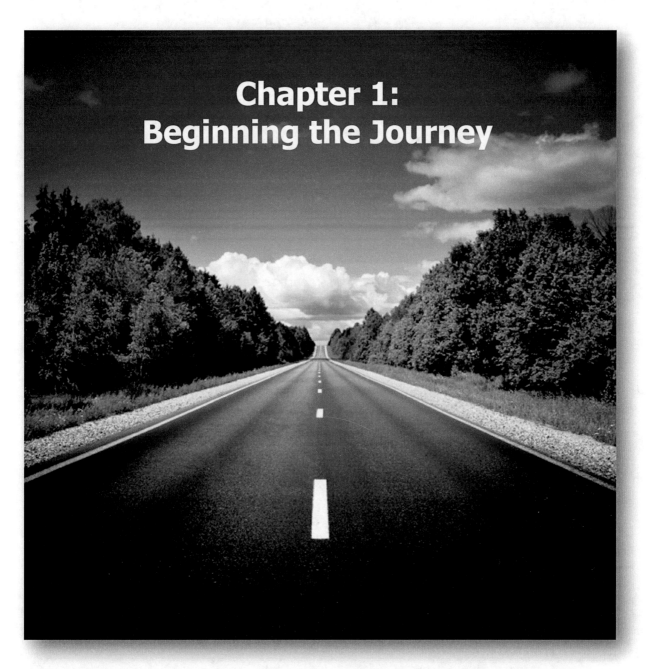

Chapter 1:
Beginning the Journey

"A happy life is one which is in accord with its own nature." ---Seneca

In this chapter you will...

- Assess Yourself
- Choose Your Major

SELF ASSESSMENT

College is a place where you will discover who you are, what you value, what you want out of life and ultimately who you want to be when you "grow up". This can only be described as a journey of self-discovery and exploration. One of the things you need to do before you transfer to a four year college or university is choose a major and the first step in choosing your major is knowing yourself.

This chapter is designed to assist you in the process of choosing the right major for you. To do this, you will start by assessing yourself, evaluating options and selecting your major. This does not have to be an overwhelming experience. The activities in this chapter will help you explore what options exist.

Why It's Important

You are getting ready to make one of the most important decisions of your life: What you will choose for a career and where you will transfer to complete your education so you are ready to start this new chapter of your life.

There are undoubtedly many people who have given you advice or expressed their expectations of you up to this point in your life. This advice was probably very beneficial in getting you to where you are today; but now, it is up to you.

- What do you want?
- What will help you achieve your goals?
- What will give you personal and professional satisfaction?

The first step is to know yourself. A clear, true assessment of who you are will help guide you in choosing the right major for your career and point you toward the prospective colleges to help you reach your goals.

Making sure there is congruency between your personality and career choice is one of the most important things you can do to ensure career happiness and success. If you like to be around people and you are sitting at your computer all day alone, this is not a good match! There are many facets to knowing yourself. These include looking at your skills, interests, personality and values.

In his text The Pathfinder, Nicholas Lore expresses a concept called the Right Livelihood. This is an ancient Asian philosophical concept that proposes a perfect working relationship and flow between you and the world around you.   "Your work fully expresses all aspects of your nature. It fits your innate talents perfectly. It expresses your temperament and personality. It provides the rewards that matter to you. It fulfills your goals. It occurs in an environment that is suitable and appropriate to who you are."   (Lore, 1998) It is when you are being you.

Ways to assess yourself

There are many ways to assess yourself and learn more about your skills, talents and your personality. These may vary depending on what decisions you have already made, how sure you are about these decisions and what issues you still need assistance with.

Check with your community college to see if they offer a career development program for students that can help you make a career decision with the assistance of a trained career counselor. These programs will help you explore and gather information about yourself and careers, so you may make an informed choice about your best career match. You will discuss your goals and expectations, use assessments to generate lists of careers, define your skills, interests and personality, and discover what you are passionate about.

Many career development programs offer career assessments such as the Myers-Briggs Type Indicator or The Strong Interest Inventory. Each assessment has its own advantages. The Myers-Briggs Type Indicator® will identify your personality type and provide a list of career fields that people with your personality type often pursue. The Strong Interest Inventory® asks questions about academic subjects and activities you enjoy and then compares your responses to people in various career fields to look for similarities. You can also access interactive free assessments through CFNC (College Foundation of North Carolina) that incorporate career information with career assessment.

Learning about yourself and your style is important not only in your college and career decisions but also in your relationships with family, friends, instructors and work colleagues. Being self-aware takes courage and the ability to see things about yourself that you may not like. But it gives you so many opportunities to live a life that is deeper, richer and more authentic. It can bring you contentment and purpose. Let's get started!

Choosing Your Major

SEPARATING MYTH FROM REALITY

The "Major" Myth: Most college students think there is a corresponding academic major for each specific career field, and that it's impossible to enter most career fields unless they choose that matching major as a student. This is not true!

The reality is that the relationship of college majors to career fields varies. Some career choices dictate that you choose a specific undergraduate major. However, most college majors don't offer specific preparation for a single type of work. The primary reason students choose the wrong major is that so many concentrate exclusively on studying for a specific "job," as if each job required a certain major. Your choice of a major is only one factor in determining your future job prospects and career path.

ASKING THE RIGHT QUESTIONS

Key Questions:

- Who am I?

- What are my values?

- What am I passionate about?

- Who do I want to be?

Students often choose their majors unwisely because they lack sufficient information about themselves, potential courses of study, the job market, and how to combine education and career goals. This is why some self-exploration is necessary. Before you choose your major, you should be asking yourself some key questions.

Begin to chart your college career, using your career goals as the basis for decisions about your academic major and minor, elective courses, internships, vacation jobs, leadership commitments, and extracurricular activities.

STRATEGIES FOR CHOOSING A MAJOR

One option is to major in something with a high potential for your human development. Another option is to consider a community college program that provides a good background for the professional areas you hope to enter in a four year university.

There is always the option of following your passion and living your dream. Or, you can develop a marketable combination of liberal arts major with a practical coursework concentration which involves the use of manual or practical abilities.

For example, a student who has dreams of owning an exclusive upscale spa and salon may choose to major in business administration at a four year university and combine that with licensure in cosmetology from a reputable cosmetology school.

EVALUATING THE MAJORS/CAREERS YOU ARE CONSIDERING

Keep in mind that, while researching and evaluating majors, you need to be realistic about what you will be required to do and what you are willing to commit to doing. In order to conduct a proper evaluation of possible majors, consider the following:

> - How many credits/courses are needed in order to graduate in that major?
> - How long will this take?
> - What is the future outlook for this major?
> - What else can you do with this major?
> - What are graduates with this major doing now?

GOING BEYOND YOUR MAJOR

Because job markets will be much more competitive when you finish your degree, you should think about going beyond your major.

- Develop skills that are immediately useful to the employer through leadership opportunities outside the classroom. Plan to gain additional experience through summer or part-time work, intern/externships, volunteer experience, extracurricular activities, and elective courses.

- Become competitive in today's market by obtaining the experience and competencies related to your chosen field.

- Avoid premature commitment to a field you don't yet understand, or single-minded concentration on one area of knowledge to the exclusion of other areas not yet discovered.

MAKING YOUR DEGREE MARKETABLE

Make your degree marketable by choosing a school with a great reputation. Establish a strong career plan. Supplement your degree with work experience and elective coursework to support your career goals. Consider combining your liberal arts degree with solid technical skills.

Quick Tips

1. **Be truthful to yourself.**
   Now is the time to take a minute and ask yourself some deep personal questions about what you want out of your life and how college can help you achieve your goals. Remember to tell yourself the truth.

2. **Take advantage of the Career Development resources offered at your community college.**
   Check to see what types of programs or assessments you can take. Make an appointment with a career counselor to discuss your career options and what majors will be applicable to that career choice.

3. **Do research about the career and major you are considering.**
   What is the job outlook for this career? Do you know how long it takes to get the degree you need? Make sure you are well informed and willing to commit what it takes to accomplish this goal.

4. **Remember you do not have to be 100% certain of your major to choose your college but it does help.**
   Knowing your major will help you choose the right college and the right program which can save you time and money in the long run.

Exercise 1.1: Your Dream Job

Your task for this activity is to think back to when you were a child. A time in your life when your imagination was vivid and bold. When you were excited about all of the great possibilities that existed for you. What was it that you dreamed of becoming one day? What job did you want to have when you were a dreamer...before the realities and limitations of life changed your mind?

Think about your past dream jobs then, think about your current dream jobs. Do this without the influence of what is or is not realistic. Don't think about money, job security, how much education is required, or what people will think. Just think about your dreams.

What are your top three dream jobs?

1. [   ]
2. [   ]
3. [   ]

Choose two dream jobs listed to complete this exercise.

1. [   ]
2. [   ]

Are there similarities between the jobs you selected? What are they? If different what draws you to two completely different jobs? Name the specific characteristics or elements that appealed to you.

[   ]

Are these jobs realistic for you? Why or why not? Are you willing to do what it takes to achieve this career at this point in my life? Why or why not?

[   ]

Consider what types of jobs are more realistic for you that are related to these dream jobs. What are some of them?

[   ]

Think about what majors relate to your dream jobs. What are those majors and how do they relate?

[   ]

Exercise 1.2: Asking Yourself The Right Questions

This is your chance to really think about who you are and how you want the world to perceive you. Read the questions below carefully and think honestly about your responses to them. Record your responses in spaces provided below. Remember, be honest.

1. Who am I?

2. What do I believe in?

3. What are my values?

4. Who do I want to be?

5. What do I really want out of my life?

6. What am I passionate about?

7. What am I good at/what skills do I have?

8. What goals have I set for myself?

9. Why did I come to college?

10. How do I want the world to perceive me?

11. What are my greatest fears?

12. What legacy do I want to leave behind?

Exercise 1.3: Evaluating Your Career and Major

The following worksheet will help you evaluate the best major for the career you plan to pursue.

Answer the following questions:

1. What is your chosen career?

2. What academic training is required for your career (Bachelor's, Master's, etc.)?

3. Is there any additional certification, licensing or credentialing required beyond a bachelor's degree?

4. How long will this take and are you willing to commit?

5. What will be your college major, concentration and/or minor for your career choice?

Visit http://www.myplan.com/majors or http://uncw.edu/career/WhatCanIDoWithaMajorIn.html

6. Describe this major.

7. What are the skills needed for this career?

8. What else can you do with this major?   List and describe at least four career titles related to this major.

Chapter 1 Reflection: Beginning the Journey

Before you move on to the next chapter, take a moment to reflect on what you discovered in this chapter and how you can apply it to your goals.

1. What are the two most important things you learned in this chapter and how will you apply those things to your goal of transferring successfully to a four-year college or university?

2. What major did you choose?

3. How confident are you feeling about your decision?

4. What do you need to do next?

**Chapter 2
Understanding
College Culture**

"Most people spend more time and energy going around problems than in trying to solve them." ---Henry Ford

In this chapter you will...

- **Research Different Types of Colleges & Universities**
- **Explore Your Individual College Needs**
- **Investigate the Best Colleges for Your Career & Major**

COLLEGE CULTURE

So you have chosen your major and now you are ready to choose the four-year college or university that you will attend to continue your education. So many decisions and options are in front of you! Should you go to a school near your home? Should you go to a public or private university? Would you prefer a large or small campus? In this chapter you will review the decision making process, explore the different types of colleges in the United States and then select the top 3 colleges for you.

College culture can be described as the combination of academic focus, language, behavior, values, philosophy and outlook that are part of a college education. It is the unspoken "rules" that college students learn to fit into a college environment. College cultures differ depending on the campus, but there are some similarities.

The first thing you should know about college culture is the change in the learning culture. In the early 1970s Malcolm Knowles introduced the United States to the concept that adults and children learn differently.

Pedagogy refers to the assumptions and strategies for teaching children. It literally means the art and science of teaching children. The theories and strategies that apply to adult learning are called andragogy which means the art and science of helping adults learn.

Pedagogy
- Applies to elementary to secondary education
- The student's learning is teacher-directed learning
- Student behavior is closely monitored / controlled
- In order to be promoted, the learner only needs to know what the teacher deems
- relevant

Andragogy
- Applies to post-secondary education
- Learning is student-directed
- Learners need to know what, how and why information is relevant to their life and
- goals
- It is assumed that the student will be responsible
- Student's life experiences become a part of the learning experience

At the collegiate level, you become an adult learner. E. C. Lindeman had five key assumptions about adult learners which were that:

1. Adults are motivated to learn as they experience needs and interests that learning will satisfy.
2. Adults' orientation to learning is life-centered.
3. The richest source for the adult's learning is experience.
4. Adults have a deep need to direct themselves.
5. People's individual differences increase with age.

(Knowles, Holton III, and Swanson, 2005)

The Different Types of Colleges in the United States
One of your current tasks is figuring out what college is the best fit for your individual, financial and career needs. In the spirit of andragogy you will be taking a close look at your personal needs and directing yourself in making decisions about which college environment you will choose to transfer to. Size, location, campus culture and cost are just a few of the factors to consider in making such a decision. Let's explore the different types of college environments that exist.

Community Colleges
- Two-year colleges offering associate degrees and certifications that focus on career readiness. Prepares you to continue getting an education or to enter the workforce immediately
- Often an affordable and convenient option

Examples: Central Piedmont Community College, Wake Tech Community College, Forsyth Tech Community College

Vocational-Technical & Career Colleges
- Offers specialized training to students who are interested in a particular industry or career
- Not required to take general education classes in all subjects
- Certificate of completion or an associate degree

Examples: Paul Mitchell School of Cosmetology, Presbyterian School of Nursing

Liberal Arts Colleges
- Most are private and focus on undergraduates
- Typically offer four-year programs leading to Bachelor's degree
- Majors include Literature, Philosophy, History, Languages, Mathematics, Humanities, and Social and Natural Sciences
- First two years general education courses; then choose a major

Examples: Wingate University, Davidson College, High Point College

Universities
- Larger and offer more majors and degree options (BS/A; MS/A; PhD)
- Most universities contain several smaller colleges
- May have to apply to a specific college within the university
- Can prepare for many types of careers or for further study in graduate school
- Can be public or private

Examples: Appalachian State University, East Carolina University

Ivy League
- Often viewed by public as some of the most prestigious universities worldwide; consistently ranked among the top 15 universities in the US
- Associated with academic excellence, selectivity in admissions, social elitism, and large endowments

Examples: Brown University, Princeton University, University of Pennsylvania, Yale University

Arts Colleges
- Focus on the arts
- Provide training in, for example, photography, music, theater or fashion design
- Most usually offer associate or bachelor's degrees in fine arts or a specialized field

Examples: California College of the Arts, Art Institute, Savannah College of Art and Design

More Types of Colleges and Universities

As you can see there many options to choose from in considering which college is the best fit for your individual needs. The challenge is for you to be truthful about what your needs are, not what others believe is right for you or what the most popular choice might be. Statistics have shown that choosing the right college has a significant impact on your success as a student and your motivation to complete your degree.

Single Gender
- Specifically for men or for women
- Historically, many US colleges were gender-segregated (until late 1860s)
- Liberal Arts, private and focus is on undergrad studies

Examples: Meredith College (Raleigh), Trinity University, Wellesley, Morehouse, Hampden Sydney

Religiously Affiliated
- Affiliated with a religious faith
- Usually private

Examples: Davidson College, St. Andrews Presbyterian College, University of Notre Dame

Special Interests
- Focus on a specific type of student population or area of interest

Examples: Gallaudet University (for the Deaf and hard of hearing), Military Institutions (Naval Academy, Virginia Military Institute)

Historically Black Colleges/Universities (HBCUS)
- Majority African American
- Programs, services & activities relevant to AA students

Examples: Johnson C. Smith University, Winston-Salem State University

Hispanic Serving
- 25% full-time population is made up of Hispanic students

Examples: Arizona Western College, Valencia College (FL)

Online Colleges
- Majority of classes offered online
- Convenience of taking class from home
- May require more coursework to compensate for not physically attending the class in person

Examples: University of Phoenix, Capella University, Liberty University Online

Public Colleges / Universities
- Funded by local and state governments
- Lower tuition for in-state students

Examples: University of North Carolina Chapel Hill, North Carolina State University

Private Colleges / Universities
- Selective admission
- Funded by private sector
- Not administered by local, state or national government

Examples: Queens University, Wake Forest University

Making Decisions

As you work through these decisions, you will want to think about your decision making style and process. How have you made decisions in the past? Are you analytical or do you go with your "gut?" Do you overanalyze and get into analysis paralysis? Do you like to talk things over with many people in your life or sit and think quietly on your own?

Throughout your college experience and life, you will be confronted with the inevitable need to make decisions. This can be an overwhelming task that if not done properly, can have unfavorable results. There is a formal process to help you make effective decisions. The Decision Making Process is the cognitive process of choosing between alternative courses of action. Let's take a look at the steps!

```
Decision-making steps:
    1. Defining the issue
    2. Investigating and analyzing the issue
    3. Developing possible solutions
    4. Selecting the best solution
    5. Translating the decision into effective action
```

Step 1—Define and State the Real Issue

This is your opportunity to define and clarify the real issue. In order to do this properly you must first determine if you are dealing with the important or relevant aspects of an issue or if you are just focusing on the visible symptoms. Problems are often the symptom and not the true problem. For example, not getting the internship of your choice (symptom) may reflect not submitting a strong application (problem); your rejection for admission to your number one college choice (symptom) may be because you waited until the last minute to work on your applications or because you did not prepare for the SAT (problem).

Take time to think about what your issue is. This is not a matter for haste, but for careful inspection and deliberation. Start to determine conditions of the ideal solution and balance long range goals. You might even find it necessary to change traditional approaches.

Step 2—Investigate and Analyze the Issue

In this step you will identify specific elements contributing to the issue/ problem that must be found and changed. Be sure that you gather all the facts and understand what they mean. Establish goals that solving the problem should accomplish and determine the requirements that the solution to the problem must meet. Ask yourself, what are the goals that resolving this issue should accomplish? This is also an opportunity to investigate and eliminate undesirable or unwise courses of action.

Step 3—Develop Possible Solutions

To begin this step, brainstorm possible options and solutions. Develop several alternative solutions for the issue and avoid "either-or" plans. This forces us to test the validity of our basic assumptions. It does not necessarily guarantee a right decision, but at least the problem has been thought through.

Remember that sometimes, to take no action at all may be one of the alternatives. This requires a decision too. However, it should not be done just to avoid something unpleasant.

Step 4—Determine the Best Solution

It is rare for an issue to have only one solution. The challenge is to select the best solution for you. Always make the best decision in light of the given facts. Consider using the technique of comparing the pros and cons of each option. This will help you think through and determine which solution seems to offer the best results with the least disturbance to your goals. Weigh your pros and cons by identifying the options or possible solutions. Then list the pros and cons for each of the possible solutions. Assign each pro and con a point value of one to five with one being the least significant and five being the most significant. Finally, total the points in both columns. The column with the most points is your best option.

Remember, even the best solution has its risks and gains. Appraise the odds of each alternative. Also, be prepared to correct the decision if new information indicates a change in status. Some questions that you might ask yourself during this step are:

- What is the potential impact this decision will have?

- Will this solution serve long-term needs?

Step 5—Translate the Decision into Effective Action

Here is where you create a plan for your decision and realize it. Consider time a factor. You should be cognizant of deadlines and be sure that it can be accomplished in a realistic period of time. Be prepared to explain your decision to those involved and affected. And always follow up to ensure proper and effective implementation as well as evaluating the effects of the decision that you made.

Quick Tips

1. **Cast a wide net.**
   It's perfectly okay to have a favorite or 1st choice for your transfer college, but choose at least five to seven other colleges to investigate as well. If you don't get into your first choice, it's always good to have a back-up plan. Don't make the mistake of only applying to your first choice and then missing out on other opportunities due to deadlines and unmet requirements.

2. **Be unafraid to apply to "fantasy" colleges.**
   You might be surprised. Apply to at least three colleges which are highly likely to admit you. Be sure to choose "safety" schools you would be happy to attend. These may be considered "safety" schools due to their cost.

3. **Look into colleges that you know little or nothing about.**
   It's a good idea to research at least two or three colleges you know little or nothing about but offer the major that interests you. Read student reviews and news articles about the colleges you are considering. It is sometimes a good idea to look outside your comfort zone.

4. **Never choose a college based on where your friends go.**
   One of the worst reasons to choose a college is because your friends go there. You can plan to visit your friend during breaks and vacations.

5. **Never choose a college based on your favorite athletic team.**
   A great football team doesn't necessarily mean a great academic program. We like to follow the teams we grew up loving but your priority when choosing a college should be academic and career related. Don't equate educational quality with name recognition.

6. **Investigate for yourself.**
   Separate reality from baseless opinions. "Hard to get into", "A party school", "Too expensive" for someone else doesn't necessarily ring true for you. Don't accept generalizations without evidence. Do your research.

7. **Don't rule out all colleges early because of cost.**
   Many colleges offer scholarships, financial aid, tuition installment plans, and student work programs that make them far more affordable. Make sure you research all financial aid options and speak to a counselor so you are well prepared for deadlines and applications that need to be completed.

Exercise 2.1: Decision Making Worksheet

Think about what issues exist that are associated with your successful transfer to a senior college/university. Then complete this worksheet based on one of those issues.

Step 1: Define and State Your Real Issue

Step 2: Investigate and Analyze the Issue

What are the specific elements contributing to the issue?

What are the facts related to this issue?

What are your long term goals related to this issue?

What is the ideal outcome?

Step 3: Develop Possible Solutions

What are two possible solutions?

Solution 1

Solution 2

Step 4: Determine the Best Solution

Complete the table below using the **two possible solutions in step 3.**   Don't forget to weigh your Pros and Cons. To do this, use the tables below to identify the possible solutions. Then list the pros and cons for the possible solution. Assign each pro and con a point value of one to five, with one being the least significant and five being the most significant. Total the points in both columns then subtract the total points for your cons from the total points for your pros to give you the total solution point value. The solution with the greatest point value is the best solution for your issue.

Table 1

Possible Solution 1:			
Pros (Advantages)	Points	Cons (Disadvantages)	Points
Total Points		Total Points	
Total Solution Point Value			

Table 2

Possible Solution 2:			
Pros (Advantages)	Points	Cons (Disadvantages)	Points
Total Points		Total Points	
Total Solution Point Value			

What is the best solution for your issue?

| |
| |

What is the potential impact this decision will have?

| |
| |

Will this solution serve your long-term needs?

| |
| |

Step 5: Translating the decision into effective action

What is your action plan?

| |
| |

By what date will you complete your action plan?

| |
| |

What are four things that you can do this week in order to translate the decision into effective action?

| 1. |
| |
| 2. |
| |
| 3. |
| |
| 4. |
| |

Exercise 2.2: College Search Evaluation

In this exercise, you will analyze and determine what characteristics of a college/university are most appealing to your individual needs. This worksheet will help you discover the best college for you based on what you value and consider most important.

Table 1: For this first activity, use the table to list and rank the factors related to your personal college needs.

Factors	Rank
Cost	1.
Location	2.
Major & Concentration	3.
Campus Size	4.
Type of College Culture	5.
Housing Needs	6.
Campus Life	7.

Table 2: For this activity, consider what you have learned about college culture so far. Use the table below to help you decide what cultural factors of a college campus you prefer. Select one of the factors listed on each row.

Type of College Culture			
	Large University	Small College	
	Public	Private	
	Co-Ed	Single Gender	
	Traditional	Online / Evening	
	Big Metropolitan Location	Small Town Location	
	Ethnically Diverse	Minority Serving	
	In-state	Out-of-state	

Table 3: List 5 colleges you consider attending. If you have less than 5, then visit: http://www.mycollegeguide.org/ to get a generalized list of schools:

A: [ ]

B: [ ]

C: [ ]

D: [ ]

E: [ ]

Table 4: In the table below, enter your score on a scale of 0-5 (5 being the best fit and 0 being no fit) to judge each feature for each school. Consider each feature by asking yourself, "Am I comfortable with this feature of the school?", or "Do I like this feature of the school?" When evaluating factual information, such as "Is my major offered?", enter a 5 for yes and 0 for no.

Sample qualities:	College A	College B	College C	College D	College E
Is my major offered?					
Distance from home					
Campus size					
Ethnic make up					
Average # of years to graduate					
City/town size and makeup					
Cost					
Gender make up					
What do my instincts tell me					
Personal Quality 1:					
Personal Quality 2:					
Personal Quality 3:					
Total School Value:					

Based on your finding, rank your top 3 college choices.

1)
2)
3)

Keep in mind that this exercise is to help guide you in the decision making process. It is not an absolute test in choosing which college you should attend.

Chapter 2 Reflection: College Culture

Before you move ahead to the next chapter, take a moment to reflect on what you discovered in this chapter and how you can apply it to your goal of transferring.

1. What are the two most important things you learned in this chapter and how will you apply those things to your goal of transferring successfully to a four-year college or university?

2. How did the results of the exercises compare to your expectations?

3. Are you confident in the choices you made? Were there any surprises or new college opportunities to consider?

4. What is the next step that you need to take?

Chapter 3
Course Planning
& Progression

"Go confidently in the direction of your dreams. Live the life you have imagined."
---Henry David Thoreau

In this chapter you will...

- Investigate degree requirements
- Learn about course planning and progression
- Complete the course progression exercise and degree checklist

COURSE PLANNING AND PROGRESSION

In the previous chapter you researched the educational requirements for your career and selected the major that will best prepare you for that career. Now it's time to take a realistic look at pursuing the course requirements for a degree in your chosen major.

One of the most significant things you will learn during this course is the importance of course planning and progression to your successful transfer to a four year college. Course planning and progression refers to the sequence of course work a student must take in order to satisfy the academic requirements of an intended degree.

Course Planning is Important Because

- It provides a clear view of the academic requirements needed to receive a degree.

- It helps you establish academic goals with a realistic date for completion.

- It allows one to evenly balance out the course work load each semester.

The concept of successful course planning is dependent on many things. Some of the most vital are being discussed in this chapter. In fact, there are three very important steps to successful course planning which include:

Step 1 Know what academic training and credentialing is required for your career field. This includes understanding:

- How course requirements relate to and vary based on your major and intended degree
- What major or degree program will best prepare you for a career in that field
- Which courses you must take to fulfill the requirements for that major
- The different levels of college degrees (see table below)

Table 1

Type of Degree	Description	Common Majors	Admissions Requirements
Certification	A designation earned by a person to assure qualification to perform a job or task.	Certified Public Accountant, Licensed Personal Counselor, Registered Nurse, Teaching, Handyman Welding	Dependent on degree earned, Exam scores, and experience
Associates (AA, AS, AFA)	Consists of general education courses and usually takes two years to complete. Majors vary depending on program interests.	Arts, Fine Arts, Science, Graphic Design, Welding, HVAC, Nursing	May have open admissions; High School Diploma required
Bachelors (BA, BS)	Undergraduate studies. 4-year degree considered the entry level degree for several fields and will have academic major attached to it.	Business, English, Biology, Chemistry, Sociology, Pre –law, Engineering, Education, Pre-med	Dependent on school and major; GPA, Scholastic Assessment Test (SAT) score

| Masters (MA, MS, MBA) | Granted to individuals who have undergone study demonstrating a mastery or high-order overview of a specific field of study or area of professional practice.

Post undergraduate level course work. Usually takes two or three years to complete. | Counseling, Social Work, Business, Psychology, Student Affairs for Higher Ed | Dependent on bachelors major, GPA, Graduate Record Examinations (GRE) scores, and Master's program |
| Doctorate of Philosophy (PhD) | Usually based on at least three years graduate study and a dissertation; the highest collegiate degree obtainable. | History, Higher Ed Administration, Mathematics, Biology | Dependent on bachelors major, GPA, Graduate Record Examinations (GRE) scores, and PhD. program |

(Table 1 Cont.)

Step 2   Understand what a college course catalog is and how to use it. This includes:

- Being knowledgeable of the jargon
- Understanding how to read and comprehend course descriptions
- Understanding the North Carolina Comprehensive Articulation Agreement

Keeping up with the academic terminology on the collegiate level can be challenging. Below is a list of some of the jargon you will hear throughout your college experience.

Table 2

The Jargon/Terms You Should Know

Major: The area of academic study in which the student focuses or concentrates. There are required courses that must be taken in order to receive a degree in a major.

Major Concentration: A focus within a major. For example, a student might choose to major in Business Administration with a finance concentration.

Minor: The secondary field of study. It must be different from the major and it requires the student to take fewer credits. Some universities have requirements for acceptance into the minor program.

Transferable Courses: College level courses that will transfer to a four year college or university. Depending on the course and the four year college's course requirements, transferable courses may or may not fulfill the general course requirements. This means that the course may only count as an elective toward your major.

General Education Courses: The basic courses required for a four year degree. These courses usually include some English, math, science, humanities and foreign languages. The number of credits required for each of these will vary depending on the college.

Elective Courses: Courses that will count as elective credits toward graduation at a four year college. These courses are not required for a major but can support another area related to your major.

Common "Core" Courses: Courses that have been identified as part of a guaranteed transfer articulation with the University of North Carolina system.

Part-time and Full-time Course Load: This refers to the number of credit hours a student takes during a semester. Your full or part time status as a student directly affects the number of years it may take you to complete your degree. The number of credits required for part or full time status varies depending on the college. A full-time college course load is usually nine to eighteen credit hours.

Open Major: A common major at the college/university in which a student is automatically admitted into upon admittance to the university. Some common majors include English, History and Political Science.

Closed Major: Students must apply for acceptance into the intended major in addition to general admission to the university. Applying to the major program usually involves adhering to additional academic requirements as well.

Terminal Degree: The highest degree obtainable for a major.

Pre-Professional Programs: Careers that require a post undergraduate degree. Examples include Law, Medicine, Dentistry, etc.

The NC Comprehensive Articulation Agreement

An agreement between the NC Community College system and the University of North Carolina system through which selected courses taught at a NC community college will be accepted by universities in the University of North Carolina system. For example, upon successful completion of ENG111, regardless of which community college teaches it, the credits will be accepted at all North Carolina state universities.

(Table 2 Cont.)

Example of a description in the course with the articulation agreement clause:

CIS 110 Introduction to Computers

This course introduces computer concepts, including fundamental functions and operations of the computer. Topics include identification of hardware components, basic computer operations, security issues, and use of software applications. Upon completion, students should be able to demonstrate an understanding of the role and function of computers and use the computer to solve problems. ***This course has been approved to satisfy the Comprehensive Articulation Agreement general education core requirement in natural science/mathematics (Quantitative Option).*** *This course is also available through the Virtual Learning Community (VLC). Emphasis is placed on MS Word, Excel, Access, and PowerPoint.*

Step 3 — Know and understand the course requirements for the colleges you are interested in transferring to and the correlation to the general education requirements at your community college.

This includes knowing:

- What type of degree you are pursuing
- What transfer degree you should be enrolled in at the community college in order to transfer to a four-year college/university
- What general education classes you need to take while at the community college
- How many credit hours are required for graduation with an associate or bachelor degree
- If your major at a four-year college is open or closed
- In which area of the college/university is your major housed
- What is the terminal degree for your major

Knowing the course requirements for your intended degree will help you plan out the courses you need to be taking at a community college which will transfer to the four-year college of your choice. The first step to making sure that you are on the right path is to be enrolled in a college transfer associate degree. This degree is designed for students who plan to transfer to four-year colleges and universities and fulfills general education requirements. Transfer degrees include Associate in Arts, Associate in Science, and Associate in Fine Arts. The degree you choose should be determined by your intended major at the university.

> **Transfer Degree Majors**
> - **Associate in Arts: Education:** Business, English, History, Liberal Arts (College courses comprising the arts, humanities, and natural and social sciences)
> - **Associate in Science:** Engineering, Pre-Medicine, Biology, Chemistry, Math
> - **Associate in Fine Arts:** Visual Arts, Music, Dance

There are many benefits to graduating with an associate degree from a North Carolina community college.
They include:

- The associate degree will transfer as a block to North Carolina public universities and other institutions that participate in the Comprehensive Articulation Agreement (CAA)
- You will be classified as a junior at a CAA university
- You will have general education exemption from any additional general education requirements of the NC public four-year university to which you transfer
- Earning your associate degree shows a strong level of commitment to finishing your bachelor degree

Although it is beneficial to complete a degree before transferring, it is not required. You can complete as few as 24 transferable hours at a North Carolina community college and be eligible for transfer admission at a university. If you are not enrolled in an associate program you should meet with an academic advisor, faculty advisor or guidance counselor to discuss your transfer options in more detail.

Quick Tips

1. **Plan early and identify requirements.**
    Learn the academic requirements for your major early and plan accordingly.

2. **Know required credentialing.**
    Know any credential requirements for your field beyond the degree for your major and make them a part of your plan.

3. **Talk to people working in the field.**
    Talk to professionals in your intended career field and find out what they majored in and seek any advice that might better prepare you.

4. **Always familiarize yourself with the course catalog.**
    Know the course descriptions at your community college and your four-year university.

5. **Know your subject strengths.**
    Are you strong in math and science or writing intensive subjects? Try to match your strengths with subjects required for your major.

6. **Balance out your academic schedules.**
    Spread your difficult subjects evenly throughout your college career to help balance out heavy course loads.

7. **Establish a relationship with a counselor.**
    Getting to know a counselor or professional at the school to which you wish to transfer can go a long way.

Exercise 3.1: Program Evaluation

Now that you have selected your major and minor, you will begin to investigate the academic requirements to graduate with a bachelor's degree in that major. To complete this assignment go to the website of your 1st choice prospective transfer college/university. Find the program/ major that you will pursue and answer the following questions.

Name of University: _____

1. List your intended major

2. Does this university offer a degree for this major (concentration and/or minor)? What is the type of degree (BA, BS, etc.)?

3. Where is this major housed at the university (department, college of, etc.)?

4. Is this major open or closed? If closed, what are the special academic requirements for admission to the program?

5. What is the total number of credit hours you have to complete in order to graduate with a bachelor's degree in this major from this university?

6. How many of the total hours must be taken in the major?

7. What is your minor or academic concentration? How many credits must be completed for this minor/concentration?

8. How many elective credit hours are you allowed to take within this major?

9. What transfer degree should you be enrolled in to transfer to this university for this major?

10. What general education classes do you need to take while at the community college?

Chapter 3 Reflection: Course Planning and Progression

Before you move on to the next chapter, take a moment to reflect on what you discovered in this chapter and how you can apply it to your goals.

1. What are the two most important things you learned in this chapter and how will you apply those things to your goal of transferring successfully to a four-year college or university?

2. Did your investigation of the academic training required for a degree in your field of interest provide you a clearer understanding of what you will have to commit to in order to obtain a degree? Are you willing to commit?

3. How confident are you feeling about your decision?

4. What do you need to do next?

Chapter 3
Paying for College

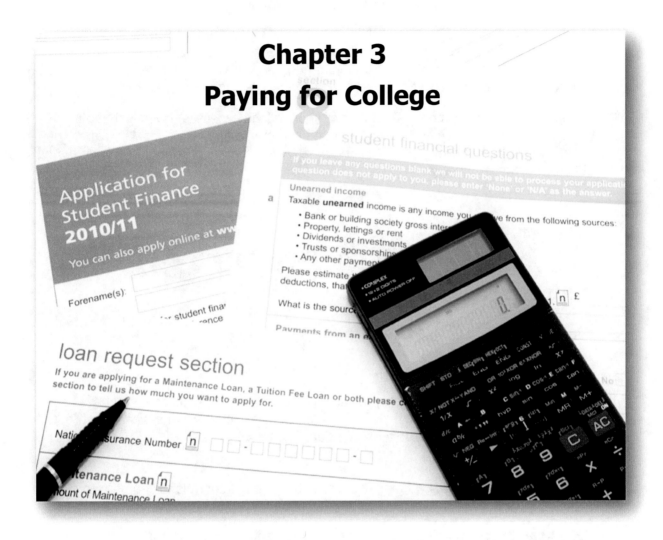

"In all realms of life it takes courage to stretch your limits, express your power, and fulfill your potential... it's no different in the financial realm."
---Suze Orman

In this chapter you will...

- Explore the Cost of College

- Investigate Different Sources Available to Pay for College

- Research Ways to Save on College Cost

- Create a Plan to Pay for College

PAYING FOR COLLEGE

Once you have decided on a career and the major that will best prepare you for that career, you will then begin to look at which four-year college or university has the program that fits your needs. In addition to the many other factors you must take into account when choosing the right college, you must also consider the cost. For many, cost is the deciding factor.

In this chapter you will research the total cost of your college expenses, investigate your options for paying, learn about ways to save on costs, and create an overall financial plan to pay for college. According to College Board, the national average cost for attending college during the 2011-2012 academic year, was:

> - Two-year Public-- $2,693
> - Four-year Public-- $8,244 (in-state)
> $20,770 (out-of-state)
> - Four-year Private-- $28,500

Associated Expenses

When you take into account how much you will have to pay to attend college, you have to consider more than the cost of tuition alone. There are many other expenses that contribute to the total cost of your education. The fees associated with these costs include, but may not be limited to:

- **Tuition & Fees:** Based on number of credit hours the student is taking per semester; may also include other miscellaneous expenses such as lab fees or student activity fees.

- **Room and Board:** Varies depending on the student living on or off the college campus.

- **Books and Supplies:** Varies depending on how many classes are taken and the required materials for each. The average yearly cost for books and supplies for a student at a four-year public college is currently between $800 and $1,100.

- **Personal Expenses:** Usually includes cost-of-living, recreation, and personal supplies. The 2011-12 national average cost for a four-year public college student living on campus is $2,066. (College Board 2011-2012)

- **Transportation:** Varies depending on how far a student must travel to and from campus, the cost of gas, bus, plane or train fare.

Colleges provide a published price, sometimes called the "Sticker Price", which includes the cost of tuition and fees, and room and board before factoring in grants, scholarships and financial aid awards. This amount is usually more than the student will actually have to pay. The "Net Price" is the total cost of tuition and fees, room and board, and books and supplies after the student has been awarded federal, state and college aid.

Terms You Should Know

FAFSA---Free Application for Federal Student Aid. This should be filed as soon after Jan 1st as possible and must be resubmitted each year. Within 4-6 weeks of completion of the **FAFSA,** the student will receive a document called the Student Aid Report (SAR), which will notify the student if they are eligible for the Pell Grant and what the family is expected to contribute to the cost of education.

CSS Profile--A supplemental financial aid application, processed by the College Scholarship Service. Some colleges and universities require the profile to calculate their own institutional financial aid awards.

SAR—Student Aid Report-summarizes information included on the FAFSA and reports the expected family contribution (EFC) and eligibility for Pell grant.

EFC—Expected Family Contribution--The amount that a student and the student's family are expected to pay toward the student's cost of attendance.

COA --Cost of Attendance -The total amount of college expenses before financial aid. Cost of attendance includes money spent on tuition and fees, room and board, books and supplies, and living expenses.

Net Price Calculator--An online tool that gives you a personalized estimate of what it will cost to attend a specific college. Most colleges are required by law to post a net price calculator on their websites.

Ways to Pay

Regardless of the amount you will be expected to pay for your college education, it's imperative that you begin thinking about ways to absorb these costs. Can your family contribute? Have you been saving for college? Do you qualify for federal student aid? Financial Aid plays a pivotal role in providing access to college as well as degree completion. It is intended to make up the cost difference between what college costs and what your family can afford to pay. It is based on the premise that all students should have equal access to a college education.

Approximately two-thirds of undergraduate students receive some type of financial aid. In 2010-2011, the average amount of financial aid that a full time undergraduate student received was $12,400.

According to the Department of Education and FAFSA guidelines, students must meet the following eligibility requirements in order to receive federal assistance:

- Be enrolled or accepted for enrollment in an eligible program;
- Have a high school diploma or GED;
- Be a U.S. citizen or eligible non-citizen;
- Not be a member of a religious community that directs the program of study or provides maintenance;
- Be registered with the Selective Service (males only);
- Not be in default on a Title IV student loan borrowed for attendance at any institution;
- Not have borrowed in excess of Title IV loan limits;
- Not owe a repayment on a Title IV grant or loan received for attendance at any institution;
- Maintain satisfactory academic progress;
- Not be enrolled concurrently in an elementary or secondary school;
- Provide a valid social security number.

If you have been convicted of possessing or selling illegal drugs, you must complete a **Drug Conviction worksheet** to determine eligibility.

Types of Financial Aid

Grants are financial aid, based on need that you do not have to repay. Grants may be given from the federal government, state government, colleges and universities, or public or private institutions.

- **The Pell Grant** is the most well-known federal aid grant in the US. It began in 1972 and is one of the key areas of funding for low income students. Eligibility for the Pell Grant is determined by family contribution, full or part time status, cost of attendance and length of study. This federal grant ranges from $602 to $5,550 for full-time undergraduate students and is available for a total of 12 full semesters of college attendance.

- **The Federal Supplemental Educational Opportunity Grant (FSEOG)** is another federal grant. This grant is intended to assist students who demonstrate exceptional financial need, with awards ranging from $100 to $400 per academic year. A student must have a Pell Grant to receive an FSEOG award.

There are also grants offered for different categories of students such as race, gender, area of study, and military background. The key is to research all the options and apply early. Many grants have a limited amount of resources and are awarded on a first come first served basis.

States also offer grants. It is important to research your state to see what grants may be offered. For example, North Carolina offers The NC Student Incentive Grant. To be eligible, you must:

- **Be a legal resident of the state of North Carolina.**

- **Be registered as a full-time student at a college within the state of North Carolina.**

- **Have proof that financial help is needed.**

Scholarships are a type of grant used to finance the cost of college. They are usually awarded to undergraduate students and offer awards that don't need to be paid back.

- **Merit-based Scholarships** are awarded for outstanding academic and/or civic achievements.
- **Need-based Scholarships** are awarded on the basis of the financial need of the student. These type scholarships will require applicants to fill out a Free Application for Federal Student Aid (FAFSA).
- **Combination of Merit and Need or Competitive** can be based on academic excellence, civic achievement, leadership qualities and athletic ability.

General scholarships have a broad nature and can be offered by any individual or organization for various amounts. Scholarships can also be program or major specific. Just remember that there are businesses and organizations in your communities that are interested in recognizing local students by sponsoring scholarships for college. It would be in your best interest to check into local scholarships. An effective search can render scholarships that are specific to a student's skills and interests.

Ways to Find Scholarships

- **Colleges and Universities** disburse the majority of scholarships available to students. A great place to search is at the four-year colleges that interest you. Also check with the department of your major. There may be scholarships or grants available to students specific to some career fields.
- **Libraries typically** reserve numerous books about financial aid and scholarship guides.
- **Advisors and Counselors** usually maintain a current collection of books and brochures on scholarships and grants. They can also be very helpful with effective application strategies.
- **Online** there are many websites available to help you find scholarships, grants, and loans that match your skills, interests, talents, and financial background. Be cautious of scholarship sites that offer information for a fee.
- **Community Organizations and Foundations** often offer scholarships to students for outstanding scholastic achievements, leadership and civic engagement.
- **Companies/Employers** sometimes offer scholarships, partial or full tuition reimbursement to their employees and the children of their employees.
- **The Federal Student Aid Information Center** at 1-800-4-FED-AID.
- **The College/University Financial Aid Office** usually has a list of all scholarships offered to the students attending that institution.

Collegeboard.org reports that almost three billion dollars in scholarships is available for college students every year. Many four year colleges and universities offer scholarships that specifically target transfer students. Make sure that you ask about the possibilities when you are researching your prospective four- year colleges.

Federal College Loans are what students and their families depend more on than any other source of financial aid. In 2010-11, 34 percent of undergraduates took out federal Stafford Loans, adding up to about $70 billion. (www.CollegeBoard.org)

Educational loans are like other loans—you have to repay the money you borrow with interest. However there are some differences in these loans compared to traditional loans. For example, you do not have to make payments while you are in college and usually start repaying 6-9 months after you graduate or stop taking classes. Also these loans traditionally have lower interest rates and you don't need a credit history to qualify.

There are three general types of loans offered:

- **Federal Direct Subsidized Stafford Loans**
  These loans are based on financial need. Subsidized means that the government will pay the interest on the loan while the student is in school

- **Federal Direct Unsubsidized Stafford Loans**
  Students get Federal Direct Unsubsidized Stafford Loans regardless of need, but will have to pay all interest charges.

- **Federal Direct PLUS Loans (Parent Loans for Undergraduate Students)**
  Parents of dependent students can borrow a Federal Direct PLUS Loan to help pay for their child's education.

Your college education is an investment that will pay off in the long run in terms of a better paying career. In the short term, loans are often a necessary option to help pay for college. The majority of college students will require student loans to help meet their educational expenses, and the average four year college graduate has over $25,000 in student loan debt. Knowing all of this, it is important to keep in mind that the amount of debt you have upon graduation can have a significant impact on your life-style after college. The question of how much to borrow needs to be very carefully considered. According to Central Piedmont Community College financial aid department, here are some tips for managing your student loan debt:

- **Do Not Over Borrow!** Borrow only what you need for your current school year educational expenses. If your expenses increase later, you can always request a second loan application up to your maximum eligibility.

- **Calculate Final Student Loan Debt Total.** Consider how much you will need to borrow to meet all of your educational goals, whether it be an associates, bachelors, masters degree, or beyond.

- **Consider monthly payment totals.** Calculate what your monthly payments will be on the loan when it comes time to repay the loan. Do you feel this monthly amount will be doable?

- **Estimate what other expenses you will have after graduation.** What will be the costs of your housing, food, transportation, insurance, credit cards, car payments, etc.

- **Consider what the average starting salary is for the career field you plan to enter.** Based on this salary do you feel comfortable with this loan debt? Also consider what the job outlook is for your career field. Where would be the best place to live upon graduation? Are you willing to move if necessary?

- **Resist the temptation** to use your student loans for other things beyond your immediate educational expenses.

The Federal Work Study Program and Student Employment

A great way to help subsidize the cost of college is to obtain employment. There are work programs available that are conducive to a college student's needs. Most any student, regardless of their financial status, can find on-campus work that coincides with their career goals. Some university programs and departments hire students as lab assistants, researchers and more. Experience working in these areas will increase your knowledge base, expand your network and help you polish your soft skills. The wages for these jobs are often competitive with the national minimum wage.

- **The Federal Work Study Program** is a federally funded employment program which provides on-campus part-time employment for students allowing them to earn a portion of education expenses while attending college. Students must qualify for financial aid in order to be eligible for this program. The colleges/universities are responsible for administering the Federal Work Study Program. Awards vary based on student need and the institution's funding level.

- **Student Work Programs** are part-time employment positions available to college students on the university campus. They too offer a competitive wage and are conducive to a college student's needs. Students are not required to be receiving financial aid in order to secure these positions.

- **Leadership Stipends** are sometimes provided to students that hold leadership positions at their respective university/college. Some leadership positions include but are not limited to those in the Student Government Association, Residence Life/Housing, New Student Orientation and Greek Life.

All of these work options on college campuses can contribute to a very rich college experience while helping you gain valuable skills that will transfer into your preferred career after college. There is also employment available outside of your college campuses but these jobs may not be as flexible with you during academic intense periods like mid-term, final exams or when you need to work on a term paper.

What Role Does Your Family Play in Paying for College

The expected family contribution (EFC) is the amount that your family is able to pay toward the cost of your college education. It is usually determined by the federal government or the prospective college. A formula uses the information you report on the FAFSA to analyze and compare your family's financial conditions with other families' financial conditions.

This formula calculates the EFC that your family can contribute by evaluating your income, assets and family size. The expectation is that a combination of savings, current income and possibly borrowing will help your family meet the EFC. The Financial Aid Office determines your eligibility for financial aid by taking the EFC number to determine a student's financial need. The formula used by the financial office is to subtract the expected family contribution from the cost to attend college (COA) to determine the student's financial need.

- **COA – EFC = Financial Need**
- **EFC calculation link:**
  http://ifap.ed.gov/efcformulaguide/attachments/010512EFCFormulaGuide1213.pdf or
- **The College Board EFC calculator link:** http://apps.collegeboard.org/fincalc/efc_welcome.jsp

Considering the family's role in paying for your college education also means having a conversation with your parent(s) or guardian(s) about the cost, what is affordable and who will pay. You need to know the family's financial status and if there have been provisions made to help pay for your education.

A great way to get the dialogue started is to inform your parents that you have decided to go to college and you would like to discuss some of your options with them. Ask for their opinion on your decision to go. This may encourage them to bring up the issue of money themselves.

Here are some talking points for the conversation about money:

- Can we afford to pay for college?
- Is there a college fund or savings committed to my education?
- Can you afford to pay the expected family contribution and how much can you afford to commit yearly?
- Are you willing to apply for a PLUS loan to help me pay for college?
- Does your employer offer scholarships for the children of their employees?
- Can I afford to attend a private college or should I pursue a public education?
- Can I afford to attend a college out of state?
- Are you aware of any scholarships from any civic or community organizations that I might qualify for?

What if Your Family Can't Help Pay for College

Parents having the primary responsibility of paying for their child's education is what federal student aid programs base a student's dependent or independent classification on. If the student is found to be a dependent they must report their parent(s) income as well as their own information on the FAFSA.

Independent status is not granted to a student living outside of the parent's home for financial aid purposes. However, there are exceptions which include:

- The event in which a student is severely estranged from their parent(s) due to an extenuating circumstance such physical or emotional abuse, severe estrangement or abandonment, etc.

In these cases the student will be able to pursue a "Dependency Override" (an appeal of the dependency status) and will need to provide 3 letters or documents confirming that validity of their claim.

According to the Department of Education and FAFSA guidelines, in order to be declared an independent, the student must provide specified documentation supporting the request for change of status.

You should also be aware that there are conditions that do not warrant independent or self-supporting status. These conditions include if the parent(s):
- Refuses to contribute to the student's education
- Refuses to provide required information
- Lives out-of-state
- Income is exhausted

Or if the student:
- Elects not to live with the parents and/or with other relatives
- Elects not to have communication with the parents
- Demonstrates total self-sufficiency

One of the strongest financial investments that you will make in your lifetime is the cost of your college education. In order to generate the best return on your investment, careful planning is a must. Remember, you must take a good, hard look at the money issues concerning the cost of college.

Ways to Reduce Costs

- Attend a Community College for your general education requirements.
- Take the maximum number of courses you can handle each semester and graduate on time.
- Consider attending a local university and commute from home.
- Buy used books or shop for reduced prices online.
- Create a budget for your personal expenses and set spending limits for yourself.
- Look for campus employment and leadership opportunities that pay stipends and offer remissions.

Quick Tips

1. **Everyone should fill out the FAFSA.**
   You should submit the FAFSA as soon as possible after January 1. Even if you think you will not qualify for financial aid due to your income, do it anyway. Many scholarships require the FAFSA to be completed as part of the application process as well.

2. **Meeting deadlines is paramount.**
   Make sure you meet any deadlines for financial aid, including scholarships and grants. Check with your college to make sure you have exact dates, including any priority deadlines. Those students who meet these deadlines are considered first for financial aid.

3. **Know what resources are available to you.**
   If you are not sure at any time, meet with a financial aid advisor at your college. Ask lots of questions. Use **www.collegeboard.org** and other websites to gather information.

4. **Find out exactly how much the college costs that you want to attend.**
   Go to the Collegeboard.com site and use their College cost Calculator. You can total up all your costs and subtract your expected financial aid. This will give you a great target of the actual out of pocket costs you can expect.

5. **Remember the 12 semester limit for financial aid.**
   Plan your courses and your finances to ensure you have enough financial aid to cover all the semesters you will need to complete your degree.

Exercise 4.1: Financial Plan for College

This worksheet will assist you in your financial planning for college. Visit www.collegeboard.org and the website for one of your top college choices to help you complete this worksheet. If you cannot find the answers to the questions on the college website, contact the college directly for an interview with a member of the financial aid staff.

I.   Name of College _____

1. What's the average cost a student at this institution pays annually for tuition and fees, books and supplies, room and board, travel, and other personal expenses combined?

2. Has there been a tuition increase in the past three years? Is there an increase expected within the next four years?

3. What are the different types of financial aid offered at this college?

4. What is the priority deadline to apply for financial aid and when are students notified about financial aid award decisions?

5. If a student is not granted enough financial aid to cover the cost to attend this university, what other options are there?

6. How does the financial aid package change from year to year (less/more)? What are the academic requirements or other conditions for the renewal of financial aid, including scholarships?

7. What happens if your financial aid package is not ready before it's time to register and pay for classes?

8. If you are not granted financial aid of any kind, how will you be billed by the college? Will you have to pay the total sum or is there an option to spread the yearly payment out over equal monthly installments?

II. Now that you have learned about the different resources available to help pay for college, what do you anticipate using?

1.
2.
3.
4.
5.

III. One of the ways to reduce college cost is to begin your journey at a community college where the cost is typically lower than four year colleges/universities. Let's start by looking and the cost you've incurred this semester and the sources from which you paid them.

Cost Description	Amount	Source/Amount	Your Contribution
Tuition Per Credit Hour X Number of Credits			
Fees required by college			
Room/Rent			
Board			
Books and Supplies			
Transportation			
Personal Expenses			
Other Costs			
Totals			

Total Amount spent This Semester	

IV. What is the breakdown of the yearly cost for your 1ST choice transfer university?

Cost Description	Amount	Source/Amount	Your Contribution
Tuition			
Fees			
Room/Rent			
Board			
Books and Supplies			
Transportation			
Personal Expenses			
Other Costs			
Totals			

Total Amount for Next Year	

V. What is the total cost for your Bachelor's degree? Total up the number of years it will take and multiply that by the cost per year.

Chapter 4 Reflection: Paying for College

Before you move ahead to the next chapter, take a moment to reflect on what you discovered in this chapter and how you can apply it to your goal of transferring.

1. What are the three most important things you learned in this chapter and how will you apply those things to your goal of transferring successfully to a four-year college or university?

2. Were there any surprises about the cost of college and your options to pay? What are they and how did they compare to your expectations?

3. What is the next step that you need to take to secure financing for college and how will you implement it?

**Chapter 5
The Admissions Process**

"You have brains in your head.
You have feet in your shoes.
You can steer yourself in any direction you choose.
You're on your own.
And you know what you know.
You are the guy who'll decide where to go."
--Dr. Seuss

In this chapter you will...

- **Research the college admissions process and requirements**

- **Review the 10 Ways to Tackle The Admissions Process**

- **Conduct an information interview**

- **Create your Admissions Campaign and timeline**

THE ADMISSIONS PROCESS

So far in this course you have selected your career and major, completed your program evaluation, and researched your financial options for the next step in your educational journey. In this chapter you will create a Personal Admissions Campaign and Timeline to use as you apply to your selected colleges. You will conduct an information interview, understand the admissions requirements for your top 3 schools and then create a tracking system to ensure you are meeting all deadlines for admissions and financial aid.

After interviewing admissions counselors and other professionals from more than 20 different North Carolina colleges and universities, we have created a list of the Top 10 Tips to consider as you begin the admissions process. Before you start your official campaign, take a look and see how these tips can make your admissions journey more successful.

10 Ways to Tackle College Admissions

1. **Visit the top two or three campuses you are interested in attending.** One of the biggest mistakes students make is not visiting a college before attending. Don't plan to make your final college selection without visiting at least your top two or three choices. You would not buy a house without looking at it, would you? How serious are you about choosing the best college for yourself?

   Sign up for a tour of the campus and ask if you can attend a class. Always take along another pair of eyes and ears and ask as many questions as possible about the college, the atmosphere and the classes. There is nothing like the gut feeling you have when you walk around the campus and talk with individuals at the school.

2. **Conduct an information interview with a member of the faculty or admissions to learn more about academic life at this college**. Some questions to consider include: What is the average class size? Are faculty teaching courses in my major or are they being taught by graduate students? Are faculty members accessible and supportive? What types of counseling, tutoring and career services support are provided here? Does the college offer any special orientation or transition support for transfer students?

3. **Talk to graduates of the colleges you are considering**. Why did they choose this college? Did it prepare them adequately for their career? What would they do differently today? Would they recommend this college's program to an individual pursuing your career path?

4. **Evaluate how successful you will be at this college**: Ask yourself: Why are you going to college? Keep asking yourself this question. How will this specific school help you build your future and maximize opportunities in your career? Are you prepared for the academic rigor and requirements to graduate? Does the college offer opportunities for extracurricular activities that support your growth as a student and community member? Can you see yourself spending time here comfortably and graduating from this university?

5. **Consider your finances.** Create a plan of how you will pay for your education. Have you applied for all financial aid and scholarships that are available? Does the college have any special scholarships for transfer students? Do you plan to live on campus? Will you be working while in college? Are there any on campus work study programs available? Planning realistically now will make you more comfortable when the final decisions have to be made.

6. **Remember that application deadlines are not suggestions.** Whether it's for admissions, SAT or ACT registration, financial aid, scholarships, or campus housing, never miss the deadlines. Missing deadlines will likely have negative results. Create a calendar and adhere strictly to all deadlines. Get organized by creating a file for each college you are applying to. Be prepared for the workload of completing your applications and gathering all the documents you will need.

7. **Start saving early for application fees.** This is often an overlooked step. You do not want to miss a deadline due to lack of funds for the application. The average application fee for colleges in the United States is approximately $40.00. Keep in mind there are many schools that will waive the fee for students with financial need, while others offer a waiver to students who apply online.

8. **Make sure you know exactly what is required for the admission packet.** What type of application must be submitted? Will you be required to apply to the college of your major in addition to general admission to the university? Do you need transcripts from your community college or high school? Is an essay required? Do you need references or letters of recommendation? Plan early.

9. **Talk to your community college professors or academic advisors about which colleges may be a good fit for you.** Choose one or two faculty who may be able to write a letter or recommendation for you if needed. The faculty should know you well enough to speak about your academic record, specific examples of how you performed in class and about your motivation and character. Be sure to follow up with deadline reminders to anyone you ask for a recommendation.

10. **When making your final choice, seek the advice of family and counselors about where you should apply.** Discuss your college options with those who know you well and whose judgment you value. They can help you sort through the options and give you different perspectives.

When it comes down to the final decision on where to apply, more than anything else, you should be yourself throughout the admissions and selection process. Think about your passion and what drives you. Show who you are and how you will contribute to the learning community at the university. Colleges want to have a variety of students from different backgrounds and varied experiences.

So let's say that you've decided to apply to transfer to five colleges/universities. Three of the five are your top choices and two that are back-up colleges just in case your top choices don't work out. Just remember that the application process can be taxing as well as exhausting. In some cases the admissions processes are designed this way to weed out those without the intellectual savvy and organizational skills to navigate their way through the process. Be sure that you develop a well-organized search and application process.

> ### To Organize Your Search
> - > **Create an electronic folder for each college to which you plan to apply**
> - > **Create a sub folder for each of the following— application, references, financial aid, transcripts, essays, housing and contacts**
> - > **Make sure that you include a check list of tasks with the correct dates and deadlines**
> - > **Update files every time you complete a task**
> - > **Always have a back-up copy of everything**

A well-organized admissions campaign will save you time and frustration as well as help you make the right decision on where to transfer.

Electronic Applications
Today most college admission application processes are electronic.

- ➢ Make sure that you have proofed and have run spellcheck on all of your information before you submit your application
- ➢ Use a secure computer to protect sensitive and confidential information
- ➢ Don't leave any blanks on the application—enter N/A for non-applicable when a question does not apply
- ➢ Protect and keep track of all passwords
- ➢ Try to finish the application in one sitting and use high speed internet connection
- ➢ Always print a hard copy of the application for your personal files
- ➢ Read through the entire application before you click submit
- ➢ Print a copy of the confirmation that your application has been received
- ➢ Once filed, check your email daily for college communications--follow directions and deadlines to the letter
- ➢ Make sure that you have respectable email addresses and voicemail messages on your phones

Transcripts

You will be required to submit official copies of your transcripts to each college you apply to for admission. This means that you'll need to make a formal request to all of your former schools—any community or four year colleges at which you have taken classes and maybe even your high school transcripts.

> Find out how the college defines the term "Official Transcripts"—usually means sealed with the college's official seal

> Find out whether transcripts must be sent directly from the college to the admissions office or attached to a transcript form

> Check the number of transcripts required from each school

> Always check to make sure that the admissions office has received your official copy

Letters of Recommendation

> Use former community college professors that can attest to your level of commitment and academic performance. Advisors for your civic/leadership engagements are strong references as well

> Get permission from your references to use them and provide all of your all pertinent information and deadlines

> Make sure you give the references enough time to complete and submit your request.

> Contact references with a reminder a week before the deadline and ask if additional information is needed

> Always send a thank you to your references

Essays

Many times when you have completed the minimum course requirement for transfer to a four- year college/university, there is no essay requirement for admission. However, you may come across a college that does require one. Admissions essays are a very important piece of the admissions process. It is an opportunity for you to show off your skills, strengths and talents.

Most colleges want to know how attending their college will benefit you and play an active role in your career and life goals. You may also have a chance to tell your unique story and motivation to pursue your career interests. This is a good opportunity for you to explain any special circumstances/ issues in your academic past. For example-- why you had low grades at an earlier time in college or why you dropped classes during the middle of the semester.

Make sure that when you are writing your admissions essay you maintain your integrity. Be authentic and true to who you are.

Remember your application is not complete until the admissions department has everything submitted. Contact the college directly to ensure that your application is complete.

Here are some additional tips for writing a strong admissions essay:

Admissions Essay Writing Tips

- *Attend a writing workshop*
- *Brainstorm ideas and create an outline before you begin the essay*
- *Open with a strong statement*
- *Always give examples that support your positions and prove your points*
- *Conclude your essay by summarizing your opening and body then state your conclusion*
- *Have a community college advisor proof your work and give you feedback*
- *Read it out loud to yourself*
- *State how your major at this college will help you reach career and life goals*
- *If necessary, show evidence of grade improvements*

How to Conduct an Admissions Information Interview

As part of your overall admissions campaign, you will be researching your top 3 colleges. You may start with online research at the school's website for some of the questions and then confirm or go into more detail as needed by speaking personally to someone from the college. You may choose to interview an admissions counselor or ask these questions when you make one of your campus visits. How you gather the information is up to you.

Listed below are some suggestions for questions to ask. Feel free to add additional questions based on your personal needs and interests.

General Information and Campus Life

1. What is the mission of the college?

2. Does the college/university accept transfer students?

3. Does the college/university have my major? Is my major accredited?

4. How many credits are required to transfer? (minimum and maximum)?

5. What is my estimated graduation date from this college/university?

6. What are the benefits to attending this college/university?

7. What is campus life like?

8. What is the demographic break down of the student population?

9. Is this a residential campus? Can transfer students live on campus?

10. What is the average class size for my major? Are classes in my major taught by faculty or graduate assistants?

11. What are some ways in which this college maintains strong connections with the work-force and community?

> [ ]

12. What sources of financial aid are available to transfer students? Do you have any special scholarships for transfer students?

> [ ]

13. What other advice would you give me in terms of admissions and transferring success-fully to your school?

> [ ]

Admissions requirements

1. How much is the application fee?

> [ ]

2. What type of application must be submitted (the Colleges app., system-wide, the com-mon Transfer app., or department app.)?

> [ ]

3. What transcripts are required?

> [ ]

4. Are references or recommendation letters required (How many?)

> [ ]

5. Is an essay required? (What is the essay topic?)

> [ ]

6. Is a portfolio required? What elements are needed or recommended?

> [ ]

7. Is an interview required or recommended? Is this in person or via phone? Is this with an individual or panel?

> [ ]

8. Is the application deadline fixed or rolling?

> [ ]

9. What's the minimum GPA requirement?   What's the competitive GPA?

> [ ]

10. Are there additional requirements to be accepted into my major?

> [ ]

11. Do I need an SAT/ACT score for admission? What is the competitive score?

> [ ]

12. What else would you like to add?

> [ ]

Quick Tips

1. **Schedule a campus visit.**
   Remember being in the physical campus environment can be the best way to get a feel for the school and decide if it is right for you.

2. **Ask questions.**
   You can talk to alumni, your professors and friends, students currently at the college and admissions officers. Talk to as many people as you can about the college options you are considering. This will help you make the most informed decision.

3. **Get clear on the admission requirements.**
   Create a file for each school and make sure you are observing all deadlines. Also give yourself plenty of time to submit a strong application. Don't force a rushed application because you waited until the deadlines were upon you to begin working on them.

4. **Make sure you have a backup plan.**
   Apply to more than one school so you can ensure you have alternative options if needed...just in case your first choice doesn't work out.

Exercise 5.1: Transfer Admissions Campaign

Your College Transfer Admissions Campaign is a systematic process course of aggressive activities and actions for the purpose of gaining admission into the senior college/university you desire. It can also be considered your marketing plan. For the purpose of this class you will be designing your own individual transfer admissions campaign.

The steps include: Naming and creating the goal for your campaign; Managing and Tracking your campaign; and Summarizing your campaign.

Naming and Creating a Goal for Your Campaign: Here you will come up with a creative name for your campaign and establish your goal. Remember, when establishing your campaign goal, you need to use the SMART method of goal setting. Make sure your goal is Specific, Measurable, Attainable, Realistic and Timely.

Campaign Name and Goal

Campaign Name	Type the name of the new campaign.
Campaign Goal	Type the name of the campaign goal.
Start Date	
End Date	
Three College Choices	
Notes	

Managing and tracking your Campaign: This involves researching the admission requirements and associated deadlines for the selected colleges. In this phase you will have to create a timeline of events to be completed for your campaign and manage those things that need to be done.

Summarizing Your Campaign: After you have researched all of the requirements for admission to your intended colleges, you will begin summarizing your campaign. In this phase you summarize your findings and make decisions based on what you have found. Once you have completed this exercise, complete the Chapter 5 Reflection based on your findings.

First Choice

Name of College:	Location:
Major/Minor:	Cost Per Year:

Admissions Requirements

Item	Required Y/N	Method	Deadline	Completed Y/N
Application(Cost)		Electronic, paper		
Test scores (number of copies)				
Official Transcripts (number of copies)				
References/ Recommendation Letters				
Admission Essay		Topic:		
Personal Interview				
Campus Housing Application				
Financial Aid Application				
Scholarship Applications				
GPA Requirement	List minimum and competitive			
Credits Required	What is the minimum number of credits required			
Notes/ Special Instructions				

Second Choice

Name of College:	Location:
Major/Minor:	Cost Per Year:

Admissions Requirements

Item	Required Y/N	Method	Deadline	Completed Y/N
Application(Cost)		Electronic, paper		
Test scores (number of copies)				
Official Transcripts (number of copies)				
References/ Recommendation Letters				
Admission Essay		Topic:		
Personal Interview				
Campus Housing Application				
Financial Aid Application				
Scholarship Applications				
GPA Requirement	List minimum and competitive			
Credits Required	What is the minimum number of credits required			
Notes/ Special Instructions				

Third Choice

Name of College:	Location:
Major/Minor:	Cost Per Year:

Admissions Requirements

Item	Required Y/N	Method	Deadline	Completed Y/N
Application(Cost)		Electronic, paper		
Test scores (number of copies)				
Official Transcripts (number of copies)				
References/ Recommendation Letters				
Admission Essay		Topic:		
Personal Interview				
Campus Housing Application				
Financial Aid Application				
Scholarship Applications				
GPA Requirement	List minimum and competitive			
Credits Required	What is the minimum number of credits required			
Notes/ Special Instruc-tions				

Chapter 5 Reflection: Admissions Process

Before you move on to the next chapter, take a moment to reflect on what you discovered in this chapter and how you can apply it to your goals.

1. What are the two most important things you learned in this chapter and how will you apply those things to your goal of transferring successfully to a four-year college or university?

2. Do you feel you have created an admission campaign that reflects your best college options with an achievable timeline and plan? Why or Why not?

3. What concerns do you have at this point about your admissions campaign?

4. Create a "To do" list of the next 5 things you need to do based on your campaign findings.

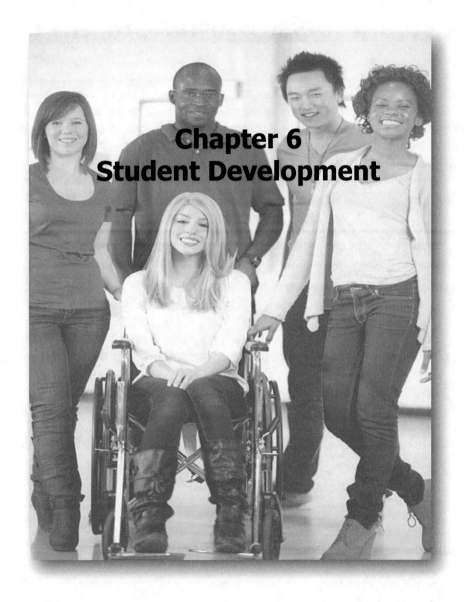

Chapter 6
Student Development

"We must live what we want the world to become." —Ghandi

In this chapter you will...

- Explore Student Development and Support Services

- Learn About the Importance of Student Leadership and Civic Engagement

COLLEGE STUDENT DEVELOPMENT & STUDENT AFFAIRS

Robert D. Brown, 50th President of the American College Personnel Association, said that cognitive and personal development on the collegiate level has been viewed as highly interlaced and that the whole student has been considered more than the educated parts. Student Affairs focuses on developing the whole student. It is the goal of promoting a marriage of the growth of intellectual development in the classroom and social development outside the classroom.

Student Affairs is a department or division of support services available to students at institutions of higher education. The programs and services are designed to enhance student growth and development for student success and degree completion. Student Affairs should work in collaboration with academic programs to provide opportunities for students to explore student life, health & wellness, leadership & service, civic engagement, and diversity.

The beginning of Student Affairs has been traced back to Athenian education and universities in The Middle Ages. In early American colleges, "in loco parentis", which means "in place of the parent", was the approach used to support students by acting as the parent while the student was attending college away from home. Through this approach, the focus was on control of the student as opposed to the modern philosophy which focuses on the development of the student as a whole. (Delworth, Hanson and Associates, 1989)

By the end of the Civil War, in loco parentis was fading out and Student Services/Affairs began to emerge. The first Student Affairs professionals with a specific function were the Deans of Women and Men and personnel workers. Student Affairs is very important to your development as a student because it can:

- Enhance student growth and development
- Promote student success and degree completion
- Ensure a richer college experience
- Help students develop skills outside the classroom

Depending on the college culture and climate, departments for Student Affairs will vary in service areas. Some of the more common areas include:

Academic and Support Services
- **Academic Advising**
  Helps students translate academic requirements established in the college course catalog into an academic plan specific to program and major
- **Admissions**
  Assists students with the processes and deadlines related to being admitted to the college/university
- **Campus Ministries**
  Provides spiritual guidance and comfort to students in need
- **Campus Police/Security**
  Provides a safe campus environment for college students, faculty and staff
- **Career Services**
  Guides and assists students with career development and workforce readiness
- **Counseling Services**
  Offers support to students facing emotional challenges

- ○ **Disability Services**
    - Works with all areas of the college to make sure that students with disabilities may independently meet the demands of college life
- ○ **Housing/Residence Life**
    - Provides on-campus housing for students with programming that promotes personal, social, educational and cultural development
- ○ **New Student Orientation**
    - Provides new students with programs and information necessary for a smooth transition and success in the college environment
- ○ **Multicultural Affairs**
    - Promotes diversity and inclusion among college students, faculty and staff

Campus Life
- ○ **Greek (Fraternity & Sorority) Life**
    - Is responsible for managing and advising the entire Greek community at the university
- ○ **Health & Wellness**
    - Promotes and advocates student physical, emotional and psychological health and awareness
- ○ **LGBTA** (Lesbian, Gay, Bisexual, Transgender Association)
    - Works to foster a safe inclusive college environment and to be an advocate for gender identity issues. Programs and services are designed to increase awareness and improve campus climates
- ○ **Recreation**
    - Is responsible for club team sports usually sponsored by the Campus Intramural or Recreation department. Men's, women's, and co-ed (men & women) teams of all different skill levels compete in a variety of sports
- ○ **Student Activities & Programming**
    - Provides campus wide programs and events that promote educational, cultural and social development

Student leadership and civic engagement

One of the most important aspects of student development is that which happens outside the classroom. Student leadership and civic engagement are arguably the most beneficial extracurricular activities a student can perform while in college. Student leadership is a learning environment that encourages hands-on experiential learning and development. Organizing and planning, critical thinking and problem solving, effective communication and working with and leading teams are some of the portable leadership skills students build while engaged in leadership and civic responsibilities.

As a prospective transfer student, it is beneficial to note that senior colleges and universities look favorably upon students that demonstrate evidence of leadership and personal development during their college experience. Here are some ways you can get involved in leadership opportunities at your college:

Student Leadership and Civic Engagement

- Student Government Association (SGA)
- Clubs and Organizations
- Learning Communities
- Fraternities and Sororities
- Service Learning

The rich experience of student leadership and civic engagement will work well for you beyond college. The skills mentioned can easily be transferred into the professional arena once you complete your college experience. In fact these are skills that companies find valuable in graduates they are considering for employment.

Students who have participated in leadership and civic opportunities often find:
- They are better prepared for the workforce
- They often become industry leaders
- They have more career marketability

For example, college students may worry because they do not always have the extensive work experience that employers are looking for when they attempt to seek employment. There are many ways to get experience that will gain the attention of hiring managers and recruiters. These include internships, co-ops, civic engagement, volunteer work, leadership, study abroad, or research with faculty. All of these are experiences that can build skills and competencies that will give you a competitive edge during the interview process.

Minimum Skills Employers Want

What skills are important to employers? In his MSU Recruiting Trends Research 2009/2010 Phil Gardner of the Collegiate Employment Research Institute at Michigan State University identified the skills and qualities that employers seek. The first 12 are essential. The New Standards also note where employers were looking for additional standards to supplement the basics.

1. Developing professional competencies and skills in your career field
2. Communicating effectively
3. Solving problems
4. Balancing work and life
5. Embracing change
6. Working effectively in a team
7. Working in a diverse environment
8. Managing time and priorities
9. Navigating across boundaries—being able to work within all levels of a company and work with members of other teams outside your department
10. Acquiring knowledge—continuing to learn and grow in your job
11. Thinking critically
12. Performing with integrity

The New Standards

1. Build and sustain professional relationships
2. Analyze, evaluate and interpret data
3. Engage in continuous learning
4. Communicate through persuasion and justification
5. Plan and manage a project
6. Create new knowledge
7. Seek global understanding
8. Mentor and develop others
9. Build a team
10. Taking Initiative

Remember that much of your development as a person occurs outside the classroom. Take advantage of programs, opportunities and services offered at your college or in your community to develop your leadership and interpersonal skills. Doing so will not only be beneficial to your career but also to your success as an individual.

Quick Tips

1. **Attend New/Transfer Student Orientation Programs.**
   As soon as you get to campus be sure to attend Transfer/ New Student Orientation. This is how you will be introduced to the college services available to you. Also establish a relationship with Student Affairs.

2. **Evaluate your academic strengths and weaknesses.**
   Identify your academic weaknesses early so that you know the areas in which you might need help and locate the office that can help you.

3. **Identify your portable skills.**
   College is a great place to build your skill set. Sharpen and improve these skills because they transition very well from college life to the world of employment.

4. **Assess and embrace your leadership style.**
   Figure out what kind of leader you are so that you'll know how and where your talents can be best utilized.

5. **Reinvent yourself.**
   No matter what type of student you have been in the past, college is a great place to become a new you. If you were introverted, become more outgoing. If you were disorganized become more focused. College is where you start to become the person that you want the world to perceive you as.

Exercise 6.1: Assessing Your Leadership Skills Exercise

To help you determine which of the skills you already possess and which need to be improved or developed, take a moment to evaluate your aptitudes. Review the list of skills below.

If you had to rate yourself on a scale of 1-5 (5 being highest/1 being lowest), how would you rate yourself?

Minimum Skills Employers Want

_____Developing professional competencies and skills and growing in your career field

_____Communicating effectively

_____Solving problems and thinking critically

_____Embracing change

_____Working effectively in a team

_____Working in a diverse environment

_____Balancing work and life/managing time and priorities

_____Navigating across boundaries—being able to work within all levels of a
            company and work with members of other teams outside your department

_____Performing with integrity

The New Standards

_____Building and sustain professional relationships

_____Analyzing, evaluating and interpreting data

_____Engaging in continuous learning

_____Communicating through persuasion and justification

_____Planning and managing a project

_____Seeking global understanding

_____Mentoring and developing others

_____Taking Initiative

○ **After rating your skills, what are your top 3-4 strengths?**

1.	
2.	
3.	
4.	

○ **What are your top 3-4 areas for improvement?**

1.	
2.	
3.	
4.	

○ **What are some leadership or volunteer opportunities you could participate in to gain more experience with these particular skills?**

Leadership or Volunteer Opportunity	Skills
•	•
•	•
•	

Exercise 6.2: Student Affairs

Visit the website of one of the senior colleges/universities that you are interested in transferring to. Once on the website, find the webpage for the Student Affairs Division and complete this worksheet.

Name of College/University: _____

1. How does the college define it's Student Affairs division and what is the mission of the university's Student Affairs department?

2. Are there any fees that students are required to pay related to the services available through this department? If so, how much is the fee and what does it cover?

3. List three academic and three social challenges that you might face at a four-year college.

4. In which areas of Student Affairs would you find assistance overcoming each of these challenges?

Chapter 6 Reflection: Student Development

Before you move on to the next chapter, take a moment to reflect on what you discovered in this chapter and how you can apply it to your goals.

1. What are the two most important things you learned in this chapter and how will you apply those things to your goal of transferring successfully to a four-year college or university?

2. What did you learn about yourself from the leadership skills assessment?

3. Do you feel more comfortable now that you know the support services available to you? Why or why not?

4. What action steps do you need to take next?

Chapter 7
Making the Transition

"Begin with the end in mind." --Stephen Covey

In this chapter you will...

- Make your final college choice
- Identify a Plan B
- Create Your Personal Mission Statement
- Prepare a Transition Plan

MAKING THE TRANSITION

Congratulations! You have researched and planned and are now ready to make your final decision on where you will continue your education. Let's take a moment to revisit the objectives for this class and the 5 Steps to Transfer Success.

Step 1
You have assessed yourself and chosen your major.

Step 2
You have explored college culture, identified your individual college needs, identified the best colleges for your career choice and major and learned about course planning.

Step 3
You then researched the cost of attending college, identified different sources available to help pay for college and learned about some ways that you can save on the cost of college.

Step 4
You explored the college admissions requirements and conducted informational interviews with your top college choices.

Step 5
In this chapter you will begin to evaluate your transfer college options, make a decision on which will be your best fit and prepare for a successful transition to your transfer college/
university.

> ### 5 Steps to Transfer Success
>
> 1. Choosing the Right Major for Your Career
>
> 2. Understanding College Culture and Your Personal Needs
>
> 3. Researching Finance Options to Pay for Your Four Year College
>
> 4. Creating a Personal Admissions Campaign
>
> 5. Making Your Choice and Making the Transition

Begin With the End in Mind

Before you make your final decision, let's step back a minute and reflect on who you are and what legacy you want to leave behind. Let's start by writing your personal mission statement.

Imagine you are 90 years old, sitting on a rocking chair on your porch. You are happy and pleased with your life. Looking back on all that you've achieved and acquired, all the relationships you've developed; what matters to you most? What would you like to be remembered for?

In his book *The Seven Habits of Highly Effective People*, Stephen Covey lists habit 2 as "Begin With the End in Mind." Often we go through life reacting to the things that happen to us and allowing other people to make decisions for us about what is important and what we should do with our lives. We may achieve great things but these can also come at the expense of things that are more valuable to us. Covey says, "If the ladder is not leaning against the right wall, every step we take just gets us to the wrong place faster."

According to Covey, "Begin with the end in mind" is based on the principle that all things are created twice. There is a mental (first) creation, and a physical (second) creation." (Covey, 1989) The physical creation comes after the mental creation similar to how a building follows a blueprint. You must make a conscious effort to visualize who you are and what you want in life; otherwise you are allowing other people and circumstances to shape you and your life by default. You need to connect to what makes you unique and then define the personal, moral, and ethical guidelines within which you can most happily express and fulfill yourself. You can use these guidelines to set your goals, make important decisions in your life and decide how you will use your time, energy and talents.

One of the best ways to ensure your life has clear direction and purpose is to develop a Personal Mission Statement. It will focus on what you want to be and do. It is your plan for success. It reaffirms who you are and puts your goals in focus. Your mission statement makes you the leader of your own life. It is the criterion by which you measure everything else in your life.

Historically, mission statements have defined the purposes of many of the world's greatest institutions and companies. For example, Coca Cola's mission is: "Refresh the world, inspire moments of optimism and happiness, and create value and make a difference." Why not use this same premise to help you define your purpose in life? Here are some strong reasons why you should invest in creating your own personal mission statement.

It can help:

- **Identify what you value:** What is important to you and what is your moral compass?

- **Identify what you believe in:** What are your principles and what do you stand for?

- **Identify your purpose in life:** What is your essential mission in life? What are you passionate about and who do you want to be?

- **Identify your personal responsibility to yourself and others:** How do you get to where you want to go and who's accountable for making it happen? What causes do you believe in? Who do you want to help?

- **Establish your personal and professional goals.** Are my daily decisions aligned with my mission? Are my goals helping me reach my mission?

A great example of a public mission statement was made back in 1960, when John F. Kennedy said that we would put a man on the moon by the end of the decade. He had a clear goal with a specific timeline for its achievement. Despite many obstacles, in 1969, Neil Armstrong had taken that one big step and helped Kennedy achieve his mission.

Writing Your Mission Statement

In her book The Path, Laurie Beth Jones says, "The truth is that all great leaders in history have had missions that were no longer than one sentence long. Abraham Lincoln's mission was to preserve the Union. FDR's was to end the Depression. Nelson Mandela's mission was to end apartheid. Mother Teresa's mission was to show mercy and compassion to the dying. A good mission statement is so easily communicated and understood that a 12 year old can understand and repeat it." (Jones, 1996)

There are many ways and formats you can use to write your mission statement. Some people write a 4-5 sentence version, some write a paragraph, and some write a one sentence declaration that they can easily memorize. Do what works for you.

- o Write a statement or paragraph that will define your purpose and mission in life
- o Consider stating the career you desire and what makes you passionate about that career
- o Think about the mark you want to make on the world and how you want to be perceived by the rest of the world
- o Consider the roles you play in your life
- o Personalize it—make it meaningful and easy to remember
- o Answer the important questions from the "Asking the Right Questions" activity
- o Be visionary and self-inspired

Mission Statement Examples

A. It is my personal mission to become an outstanding physician of Obstetrics and Gynecology and surgeon. I wish to return to my home in Djibouti to provide effective medical treatment to women whom have suffered from female genital mutilation. I want to help restore the spirit and heal the wounds of victims of violent crimes against women. I also endeavor to fight to have the practice of FMG abolished in my country and the world. (Mission Statement of ACA 122 student at CPCC, Fall 2010)

B. Anonymous example of a mission statement:

- My mission is to give, for giving is what I do best and I can learn to do better.

- I will seek to learn, for learning is the basis for growth, and growing is the key to living. I will seek first to understand, for understanding is the key to finding value, and value is the basis for respect, decisions, and action. This should be my first act with my wife, my family, and my business.

- I want to help influence the future development of people and organizations. I want to teach my children and others to love and laugh, to learn and grow beyond their current bounds.

- I will build personal, business, and civic relationships by giving, in frequent little ways.

What do we do with it?

- **Take pride and ownership in your personal mission statement.** Put it on display or in a special place. You should look at it weekly to keep yourself motivated and on track.

- **Allow humble self-analysis of your personal growth and development.** Use this to reflect on what yet needs to be done and the achievements accomplished to this point in time.

- **Always allow room for revising**. As life's experiences provoke growth and change, expect to make adjustments to your goals and desires, as they will shift with age.

Making the Right Decision

Once you have been accepted to one or more of the colleges to which you have applied, you will be faced with the big decision of which is the best college for you. If needed, refer back to the decision making worksheet (Chapter 2) to help you to make the right decision. To also help you with this, evaluate the following factors:

➢ How do you feel about the college in general?
➢ Is this the right college culture?
➢ What's the size of the student body? Is the campus size ideal?
➢ Did you get accepted into your major?
➢ How large or small are the classes?
➢ How many of your community college credits will this college accept?
➢ When will you be able to graduate?
➢ Did you visit the campus and how was it?
➢ How much financial aid and scholarships will you get?
➢ How much out of pocket cost is involved?
➢ What is the housing situation? Will it fit your needs?

Get an official report of the credits that will transfer

With the cost of college being so expensive today you need to have a clear understanding of exactly how many college credits you have remaining and how many years it will take you to graduate. Before you make your decision to attend any of the colleges that you've been accepted to, you need to request an official report of which courses you will get credit for from your community college, and how they will count toward your major, general education requirements or electives.

Don't be afraid to negotiate any courses that are not accepted at the four year university. You might be surprised at how far a well-researched justification can get you. Always look at the course descriptions and compare to the descriptions of the classes you have taken. You may be able to convince the advisor to consider the option for a course requirement or as an elective.

What is your Plan B?

Considering that the demand for jobs today promotes an employer's market, it would behoove any student to pursue studies at the universities with strongest programs for your major in the state and in some cases the nation. Sometimes despite your best efforts, things don't work out as you planned. In such cases, everyone should have a "Plan B". Plan B is a popular term used to mean a reserved, secondary plan, in case a first plan (a hypothetical 'Plan A') fails.

➢ Apply to more than your top transfer college choices. Have at least two to three fall back options.
➢ Sometimes if you don't get in on your first try you can take courses at the college to demonstrate that you can handle the work load then stress your efforts when you reapply.

College Road Map

As you think about the next 2-4 years, the following checklist will prove helpful to you in terms of planning the key activities you may want to do each year to prepare for your life after college. This document is designed to work as a guide toward your college success. Feel free to add additional items that may pertain to your individual collegiate journey.

First Year: Acclimating Yourself to College Life

- Set goals for the year.
- Get to know yourself and how you fit into college life.
- Explore your academic and extracurricular interests.
- Adjust to your new environment and the freedom/responsibility that go along with it.
- Assess your study skills and habits – improve them if they need work.
- Figure out the difference in the academic demands from your previous school and find resources that will contribute to your success.
- Explore clubs and organizations that interest you.
- Talk to other students for advice about their majors, classes and professors.
- Start to become aware of people in roles who are doing work that is interesting to you.
- Consider a job, an internship or a volunteer experience in an area that interests you.
- Begin researching career and major possibilities.
- Enroll in a transfer degree program.
- Begin researching prospective senior colleges and request admissions information.

Second Year: Exploring Careers and Majors

- Set goals for the year.

- Meet with your faculty advisor to discuss majors and course planning options. Establish your academic plan.

- Establish a strong relationship with career services and find out what insights they provide on career direction. Map out your career plan. Conduct a more detailed exploration of occupations and possibilities. Identify possible career field options.

- Learn how to network and cultivate mentors. Start attending networking events. Create a tracking system for your contacts. Attend career fairs and workshops and start making contacts.
- Conduct informational interviews with people working in career fields that interest you.
- Get more invested in leadership opportunities and extracurricular activities. Find out what organizations related to your career/major exist. Consider running for an executive position within an organization.
- Start exploring service learning/volunteer opportunities. Get hands-on experience by using your breaks and vacations to volunteer and intern.
- Select your major and concentration or minor.
- Keep a journal of your experiences and the skills you are gaining while in college.
- Begin looking into graduate schools and requirements (exams, GPA requirements, costs, fellowships etc.).
- Decide on the transfer colleges you will apply to.
- Meet with your faculty advisor to make sure you are on schedule to graduate/transfer.
- Conduct campus visits for top college transfer choices.
- Plan living arrangements for next year.
- Apply for graduation at your community college.

Third Year: Building Your Marketing Plan
- Set goals for career related interning, externing, volunteering, and summer job experience. Everything that you do should be geared toward the career path you've chosen. Talk to prospective employers about possible jobs and internships and be willing to accept non-paying positions.
- Prioritize your interests and begin creating your career marketing plan. Build a portfolio
- Choose academic electives that enhance your learning and career goals.
- Get a head start on preparing for grad school admissions processes. Take any grad school exams (LSAT, MCAT, GRE etc.). This will allow time to retake if needed.
- Conduct career research. Target and research potential employers/companies and areas that you wish to pursue your career with.
- Hone your job search skills and techniques (communication, interpersonal, research, networking, interviewing). Start working closely with career services to create a solid resume and get it out there. Practice and improve your interviewing skills. Start working on your interview attire. Update resume to reflect current experiences.
- ☐ Increase your networking skills.
- ☐ Start connecting with alumni in your field of interest.
- ☐ Reassess your extracurricular activities. Look for more challenging opportunities.
- ☐ Continually refine your job search or graduate school plans.
- ☐ Plan your senior year and create a To Do/Check List. This will help to minimize possible stress during your senior year.

Fourth Year: Transitioning to Life After College
- ☐ Meet with your advisor to make sure that you're on track to graduate this year.
- ☐ Apply for graduation.
- ☐ Network and make the most of all of your college's career fairs, forums, and employment readiness workshops. Consider volunteering for some of the events to get the inside track.

- Research potential employers. Identify relevant periodicals and trade journals. Bone up on new trends in your specialty area. Develop a job search strategy.
- Visit career services. Brush up on your interviewing skills and refine your resume.
- Get your interviewing attire together.
- Clean up your online image. Make sure you Google yourself and check your Facebook, Twitter and other online profiles.
- Apply to graduate school if you're planning to go.
- Make contact with your references, get their permission to use their names and obtain the correct contact information for them.
- Plan to make your transition to life after college. Where will you live? How will you get to work? What if the job you really want doesn't work out? What is your back-up plan?
- Take your finals and graduate!

Transitioning Successfully

You have now made your final decision on where you will finish your education. Do you have an action plan for the next few critical steps you need to take? Here is a list of items that you should be sure to complete once you have decided which transfer college/university you will attend.

- Use the formal process of accepting admission to notify the four year college/university in writing that you have decided to attend.
- Have an official copy of your final grades sent to your transfer college/university.
- Contact campus housing to reserve your space.
- Contact your new faculty advisor for your major to schedule your first official advising session.
- Contact the admissions and the college business office to find out when tuition and fees, housing deposits are due and how they must be paid.
- Sign up for New and Transfer Student Orientation.

Take a minute to work through the table below of the next 3-5 tasks you need to complete as you begin your transfer process. There are some ideas listed below to get you started. Also, try to incorporate applicable tasks from the college road map. You can complete your own transition plan on Exercise 7.2 at the end of this chapter.

Table 1: Transfer Task List

Action Item	Dates	Notes	Complete/ Incomplete
Attend community college and receive a _____ degree.	August 2013-May 2015		
I will transfer to _____ where I will major in _____.	August 2015—May 2017		
Attend transfer student orientation.			

What If It Doesn't Work Out?

It is possible that you may get to your senior university and things may not work out as planned. Maybe you have issues with your finances, family obligations or other life events that prevent you from completing your education at that school. Make sure that before you choose to leave that you exhaust every effort to make it work. Try using some of the student support services available to you at the university. For academic issues, meet with your professor and look into tutoring. For financial issues you may want to look into part-time work or unclaimed scholarships. If you have trouble with your roommate or living in the residence halls, the Housing Office can help you resolve roommate conflicts or secure other housing arrangements.

If none of these resolve your issue and you find that it is best to leave, don't feel like a failure. Take whatever steps you need to take to exit that institution with dignity and go to your Plan B scenario. Take care to ensure you have withdrawn from your courses if necessary and spoken to your advisors and counselors. You will want to make sure you leave in good standing and that such good standing is reflected on your academic record. You can then take your experiences, learn from those and move to your Plan B as soon as you are able. Also, find out if you are eligible for a refund of your tuition and fees. The money can help you get started on Plan B.

Final Thoughts

Our journey to transferring successfully has come to an end. But in reality this is just the beginning: The beginning of a new chapter in your life, your mission and your educational journey. We hope that the information and techniques learned in this course will provide you with the knowledge and confidence to successfully transition into a four-year college/university environment.

Additionally, we hope that this transition will help bring to fruition your goals of graduating with a bachelor's degree and your successful entry into the career of your choosing and living your best life. While you will have many people you can go to for advice such as advisors, counselors, friends and family, we hope you will realize that you have the power to create the kind of future you want.

"Your time is limited, so don't waste it living someone else's life. Don't let the noise of others' opinions drown out your own inner voice. And most important, have the courage to follow your heart and intuition." Steve Jobs

.

Quick **Tips**

In the textbook, College Student Success, Bazan, J., Bazan, L., Dunham and Johnson have outlined the following **"Success Strategies in College"** to help you flourish in college:

1. **Show up.**
   The very first day of class, be there. No matter who tells you that it doesn't matter if you attend the first day or week, that advice is wrong.

2. **Be prepared.**
   Be prepared to give your full, uninterrupted attention to the dynamics of the class so that you can extract the important information you need for discussions and future exams.

3. **Take notes.**
   Even if you are an auditory learner, you can benefit from the kinesthetic and visual experience of taking notes in class.

4. **Plan ahead.**
   Figure out what you want to do, what classes you want and need, and which instructors will teach to your learning style.

5. **Check a limiting attitude at the door.**
   Some of these attitudes may unnecessarily limit your opportunity for success.

6. **Become involved.**
   Students who sit in the front of the class are more likely to be involved in lecture, classroom discussions and activities.

7. **Get to know your instructor.**
   One of the best ways to become successful in any course is to get to know your instructor.

8. **Don't procrastinate.**
   Instructors can usually distinguish the work that's done with care and precision from work thrown together at the last minute. That's why some students get "A"s and "B"s and some get "C"s, "D"s, and "F"s.

9. **Don't ask if you missed anything after missing a week's worth of classes.**
   Even if you just missed a day, you missed something. It was important. It may or may not be on the test, but it was still important. You are responsible for work you miss.

10. **Speaking of "Will it be on the test?"**
    In most classes everything is fodder for the test. If you have followed the previous nine suggestions, however, and practice student success strategies, you should be able to recognize most of the likely exam topics.

Exercise 7.1: Create Your Own Personal Mission Statement

Now that you have an idea of what a personal mission statement is and how it is designed, you will create your own. Refer back to your responses to the "Asking Yourself the Right Questions" worksheet for inspiration and create a four to five sentence personal mission statement.

Your Personal Mission Statement:

```

```

Next you will establish one long-term goal, two mid-term and two short-term goals that support and are directly related to your personal mission statement. Remember, a long-term goal is a goal to be accomplished in five or more years. A mid-term goal can be accomplished in one to five years and a short-term goal can be accomplished in one year or less. Think of this task in terms of your long-term goal being related to your career and your mid-term goals being related to the education that will help prepare you for this career. Your short-term goals should be related to your semester here at the community college or your next semester. Focus on using the S.M.A.R.T. process when establishing your goals. This means goals must be specific, measurable, attainable, realistic and timely.

Long-term Goals:

1.
2.

Mid-term Goals:

1.
2.

Short-term Goals:

1.
2.

As you look back on your personal mission statement and goals, what are some tasks that you can commit to doing this week in order to be successful in accomplishing your goals?

How is the selection of your #1 college going to help you achieve your mission?

Exercise 7.2: Transfer Task List

You have now made your final decision on where you will finish your education. Do you have an action plan for the next few critical steps you need to take? Take a minute to work through the table below of the next 3-5 tasks you need to complete as you begin your transfer process.

Action Item	Dates	Notes	Complete/ Incomplete

Chapter 7 Reflection: Making the Transition

Before you move on to the next chapter, take a moment to reflect on what you discovered in this chapter and how you can apply it to your goals.

1. What is the benefit of establishing your mission and goals? How can this apply to your educational endeavors and to your life after college?

2. After taking this class, do you feel better prepared to successfully transition to a four-year college/university? Why?

3. What are the three most beneficial things that you learned in this class?

4. What are 3 things you can do once you are at a four-year college to ensure your successful degree completion?

References

Books

Bazan, James, Laura Bazan, Linda Dunham & Elvira Johnson. (2012). College Student Success. Charlotte: CPCC Press.

Covey, Stephen. (1989). The 7 Habits of Highly Effective People. New York: Simon & Schuster.

Delworth, Hanson and Associates. (1989). Student Services, Second Edition. San Francisco: Jossey-Bass Inc.

Hartman, Kathleen. (2008). 35 Ways to Discover A Major. Boston: Houghton-Mifflin Company.

Jones, Laurie Beth. (1996). The Path: Creating Your Mission Statement for Work and Life. New York: Hyperion.

Knowles, Malcolm S. Ph.D., Elwood F. Holton III Ed.D. and Richard A. Swanson Ph.D. (2005). The Adult Learner, Sixth Edition: The Definitive Classic in Adult Education and Human Resource Development. San Diego: Elsevier.

Lore, Nicholas. (1998). The Pathfinder: How to Choose or Change your Career for a Lifetime of Satisfaction and Success. New York: Simon & Schuster.

O'Shaughnessy, Lynn. (2008). The College Solution. New Jersey: FT Press

Silver, Don. 2010. Community College Transfer Guide. Los Angeles: Adams-Hall Publishing

Articles

Choi, Candice, Pope, Justin. "What Does College Really Cost?". Charlotte Observer: Business. (Oct. 16, 2011)

Gardner, Phil. "MSU Recruiting Trends Research 2009/2010"; Collegiate Employment Research Institute, Michigan State University. (2010)

Websites

http://www.cpcc.edu/financial_aid
http://www.cfnc.org

http://www.petersons.com

http://www.collegeboard.org

http://www.usnews.com/education/worlds-best-universities-rankings